Learning System

Cram101 Textbook Outlines is a learning system. The notes in this book are the highlights of your textbook, you will never have to highlight a book again.

How to use this book. Take this book to class, it is your notebook for the lecture. The notes and highlights on the left hand side of the pages follow the outline and order of the textbook. All you have to do is follow along while your instructor presents the lecture. Circle the items emphasized in class and add other important information on the right side. With Cram101 Textbook Outlines you'll spend less time writing and more time listening. Learning becomes more efficient.

Cram101.com Online

Increase your studying efficiency by using Cram101.com's practice tests and online reference material. It is the perfect complement to Cram101 Textbook Outlines. Use self-teaching matching tests or simulate in-class testing with comprehensive multiple choice tests, or simply use Cram's true and false tests for quick review. Cram101.com even allows you to enter your in-class notes for an integrated studying format combining the textbook notes with your class notes.

Visit **www.Cram101.com**, click Sign Up at the top of the screen, and enter **DK73DW16569** in the promo code box on the registration screen. Your access to www.Cram101.com is discounted by 50% because you have purchased this book. Sign up and stop highlighting textbooks forever.

Nursing Theory: Utilization & Application
Martha Raile Alligood, 1st

CONTENTS

Chapter 1. The Nature of Knowledge Needed for Nursing Practice,

Nursing	Nursing is a healthcare profession focused on the care of individuals, families, and communities so they may attain, maintain, or recover optimal health and quality of life from conception to death.
	Nurses work in a large variety of specialties where they work independently and as part of a team to assess, plan, implement and evaluate care. Nursing Science is a field of knowledge based on the contributions of nursing scientist through peer reviewed scholarly journals and evidenced-based practice.
Knowledge	Knowledge is defined by the Oxford English Dictionary as (i) expertise, and skills acquired by a person through experience or education; the theoretical or practical understanding of a subject; (ii) what is known in a particular field or in total; facts and information; or (iii) be absolutely certain or sure about something. Philosophical debates in general start with Plato's formulation of knowledge as "justified true belief." There is however no single agreed definition of knowledge presently, nor any prospect of one, and there remain numerous competing theories. Knowledge acquisition involves complex cognitive processes: perception, learning, communication, association and reasoning.
Ambulatory care	Ambulatory care is any medical care delivered on an outpatient basis. Many medical conditions do not require hospital admission and can be managed without admission to a hospital. Many medical investigations can be performed on an ambulatory basis, including blood tests, X-rays, endoscopy and even biopsy procedures of superficial organs.
Ambulatory care nursing	Ambulatory care nursing is characterized by rapid, focused assessments of patients, long-term nurse/patient/family relationships and teaching and translating prescriptions for care into doable activities for patients and their caregivers.
	Ambulatory care nurses work in outpatient settings, responding to high volumes of patients in short term spans while dealing with issues that are not always predictable. The specialty spans all populations of patients, and care ranges from wellness/prevention to illness and support of the dying.

Chapter 1. The Nature of Knowledge Needed for Nursing Practice,

Chapter 1. The Nature of Knowledge Needed for Nursing Practice,

Education	Education in the largest sense is any act or experience that has a formative effect on the mind, character or physical ability of an individual. In its technical sense, education is the process by which society deliberately transmits its accumulated knowledge, skills and values from one generation to another.
	Etymologically, the word education is derived from educare "bring up", which is related to educere "bring out", "bring forth what is within", "bring out potential" and ducere, "to lead".
Skill	A Skill is the learned capacity to carry out pre-determined results often with the minimum outlay of time, energy, or both. Skills can often be divided into domain-general and domain-specific Skills. For example, in the domain of work, some general Skills would include time management, teamwork and leadership, self motivation and others, whereas domain-specific Skills would be useful only for a certain job.
Healing	Physiological healing is the restoration of damaged living tissue to normal function. It is the process by which the cells in the body regenerate and repair to reduce the size of a damaged or necrotic area. Healing incorporates both the removal of necrotic tissue (demolition), and the replacement of this tissue.
Nursing research	Nursing research is the term used to describe the evidence used to support nursing practice. Nursing, as an evidence based area of practice, has been developing since the time of Florence Nightingale to the present day, where many nurses now work as researchers based in universities as well as in the health care setting.
	Nurse education places emphasis upon the use of evidence from research in order to rationalise nursing interventions.
Nurse	A Nurse is a healthcare professional who, in collaboration with other members of a health care team, is responsible for: treatment, safety, and recovery of acutely or chronically ill individuals; health promotion and maintenance within families, communities and populations; and, treatment of life-threatening emergencies in a wide range of health care settings. Nurses perform a wide range of clinical and non-clinical functions necessary to the delivery of health care, and may also be involved in medical and nursing research.

Chapter 1. The Nature of Knowledge Needed for Nursing Practice,

Both Nursing roles and education were first defined by Florence Nightingale, following her experiences caring for the wounded in the Crimean War.

Training

The term Training refers to the acquisition of knowledge, skills, and competencies as a result of the teaching of vocational or practical skills and knowledge that relate to specific useful competencies. It forms the core of apprenticeships and provides the backbone of content at institutes of technology . In addition to the basic Training required for a trade, occupation or profession, observers of the labor-market recognize today the need to continue Training beyond initial qualifications: to maintain, upgrade and update skills throughout working life.

Nursing theory

Nursing theory is the term given to the body of knowledge that is used to define or explain various aspects of the profession of nursing.

Types of nursing theories

Grand nursing theories

Grand nursing theories have the broadest scope and present general concepts and propositions. Theories at this level may both reflect and provide insights useful for practice but are not designed for empirical testing.

Orthopedic

Orthopedic surgery or Orthopedics (also spelled orthopaedics) is the branch of surgery concerned with conditions involving the musculoskeletal system. Orthopedic surgeons use both surgical and non-surgical means to treat musculoskeletal trauma, sports injuries, degenerative diseases, infections, tumors, and congenital conditions.

Nicholas Andry coined the word `orthopaedics`, derived from Greek words for orthos and paideion (`child`), when he published Orthopaedia: or the Art of Correcting and Preventing Deformities in Children in 1741.

Osteoporosis

Osteoporosis is a disease of bone that leads to an increased risk of fracture. In Osteoporosis the bone mineral density (BMD) is reduced, bone microarchitecture is disrupted, and the amount and variety of non-collagenous proteins in bone is altered. Osteoporosis is defined by the World Health Organization (WHO) in women as a bone mineral density 2.5 standard deviations below peak bone mass (20-year-old healthy female average) as measured by DXA; the term `established Osteoporosis` includes the presence of a fragility fracture.

Chapter 1. The Nature of Knowledge Needed for Nursing Practice,

Outcome	In game theory, an outcome is a set of moves or strategies taken by the players, or their payoffs resulting from the actions or strategies taken by all players. The two are complementary in that, given knowledge of the set of strategies of all players, the final state of the game is known, as are any relevant payoffs. In a game where chance or a random event is involved, the outcome is not known from only the set of strategies, but is only realized when the random event(s) are realized.
Accreditation	Accreditation is a process in which certification of competency, authority, or credibility is presented. Organizations that issue credentials or certify third parties against official standards are themselves formally accredited by Accreditation bodies (such as UKAS); hence they are sometimes known as 'accredited certification bodies'. The Accreditation process ensures that their certification practices are acceptable, typically meaning that they are competent to test and certify third parties, behave ethically, and employ suitable quality assurance.
Utilization	Utilization is a statistical concept (Queueing Theory) as well as a primary business measure for the rental industry. In queueing theory, utilization is the proportion of the system`s resources which is used by the traffic which arrives at it. It should be strictly less than one for the system to function well.
Evidence-based practice	· Epidemiology · Evidence-based design · Evidence-based management · Evidence-based medicine · Evidence-based pharmacy in developing countries · Dynamic treatment regimes

Chapter 1. The Nature of Knowledge Needed for Nursing Practice,

· Dale AE (2005). `Evidence-based practice: compatibility with nursing`. Nurs Stand 19 (40): 48-53.

Nursing practice

Nursing practice is the actual provision of nursing care. In providing care, nurses are implementing the nursing care plan which is based on the client's initial assessment. This is based around a specific nursing theory which will be selected as appropriate for the care setting.

Primary

In medicine, the reporting of symptoms by a patient may have significant psychological motivators. Psychologists sometimes categorize these motivators into primary or secondary gain.

primary gain is internally good; motivationally.

Primary care

Primary care is the term for the health services which play a central role in the local community. It refers to the work of health care professionals who act as a first point of consultation for all patients. Such a professional would usually be a general practitioner or family physician, depending on locality.

Humans

Humans commonly refers to the species Homo sapiens , the only extant member of the Homo genus of bipedal primates in Hominidae, the great ape family. However, in some cases the term is used to refer to any member of the genus Homo.

Humans have a highly developed brain, capable of abstract reasoning, language, introspection, and problem solving.

Customer

A customer buyer, is usually used to refer to a current or potential buyer or user of the products of an individual or organization, called the supplier, seller, or vendor. This is typically through purchasing or renting goods or services. However, in certain contexts, the term customer also includes by extension anyone who uses or experiences the services of another.

Chapter 2. Nursing Models: Normal Science for Nursing Practice,

Normal

- normal, Alabama

- normal, Illinois

- normal a film starring Jessica Lange and Tom Wilkinson

- normal a film by Carl Bessai

- normal or Angels Gone, a Czech film

- normal, a character on Dark Angel

- The normal, a band featuring Daniel Miller

- `normal`, a song by Foo Fighters

- `normal`, a song by Porcupine Tree

- `normal`, a song by The Exies

- normality (concentration), the discrepancy between the concentrations of ionic species in a solution

- Surface normal, a vector (or line) that is perpendicular to a surface

- normal component, the component of a vector that is perpendicular to a surface

- normal curvature, of a curve on a surface, the component of curvature that is normal to the surface

- normal distribution, a type of probability distribution in probability theory and statistics

Chapter 2. Nursing Models: Normal Science for Nursing Practice,

· normal extension, in abstract algebra, a certain type of algebraic field extensions

· normal equations, for linear least squares, a model fitting technique using projection matrices

· normal family, a pre-compact family of holomorphic functions

· normal function, a continuous strictly increasing function from ordinals to ordinals

· normal matrix, a matrix which commutes with its conjugate transpose

· normal measure, a particular type of measure on a measurable cardinal

· normal mode, a special type of solution in an oscillating system

· normal morphism, is a morphism that arises as the kernel or cokernel of some other morphisms

· normal number (computing), a number that is within the normal range of a floating-point format

· normal number, a number whose digit sequence is random

· normal operator, a linear operator on a Hilbert space that commutes with its adjoint

· normal polytope, a lattice polytope in which dilation of points is given by summing lattice points

· normal ring, a ring that is its own integral closure in its field of fractions

· normal space, a topological space in which disjoint closed sets can be separated by disjoint neighborhoods

· normal subgroup, a subgroup that is invariant under conjugation in abstract algebra

· normal point, a point on a variety whose local ring is integrally closed

Chapter 2. Nursing Models: Normal Science for Nursing Practice,

	· normal forms, in database normalization, criteria for determining a table's degree of vulnerability to logical inconsistencies .
Nursing	Nursing is a healthcare profession focused on the care of individuals, families, and communities so they may attain, maintain, or recover optimal health and quality of life from conception to death.
	Nurses work in a large variety of specialties where they work independently and as part of a team to assess, plan, implement and evaluate care. Nursing Science is a field of knowledge based on the contributions of nursing scientist through peer reviewed scholarly journals and evidenced-based practice.
Nursing theory	Nursing theory is the term given to the body of knowledge that is used to define or explain various aspects of the profession of nursing.
	Types of nursing theories
	Grand nursing theories
	Grand nursing theories have the broadest scope and present general concepts and propositions. Theories at this level may both reflect and provide insights useful for practice but are not designed for empirical testing.
Utilization	Utilization is a statistical concept (Queueing Theory) as well as a primary business measure for the rental industry.
	In queueing theory, utilization is the proportion of the system's resources which is used by the traffic which arrives at it. It should be strictly less than one for the system to function well.
Health	At the time of the creation of the World Health Organization (WHO), in 1948, Health was defined as being `a state of complete physical, mental, and social well-being and not merely the absence of disease or infirmity`.

Chapter 2. Nursing Models: Normal Science for Nursing Practice,

This definition invited nations to expand the conceptual framework of their Health systems beyond issues related to the physical condition of individuals and their diseases, and it motivated us to focus our attention on what we now call social determinants of Health. Consequently, WHO challenged political, academic, community, and professional organizations devoted to improving or preserving Health to make the scope of their work explicit, including their rationale for allocating resources.

Health care

Health care , refers to the treatment and management of illness, and the preservation of health through services offered by the medical, dental, complementary and alternative medicine, pharmaceutical, clinical laboratory sciences , nursing, and allied health professions. Health care embraces all the goods and services designed to promote health, including `preventive, curative and palliative interventions, whether directed to individuals or to populations`.

Before the term Health care became popular, English-speakers referred to medicine or to the health sector and spoke of the treatment and prevention of illness and disease.

Humans

Humans commonly refers to the species Homo sapiens , the only extant member of the Homo genus of bipedal primates in Hominidae, the great ape family. However, in some cases the term is used to refer to any member of the genus Homo.

Humans have a highly developed brain, capable of abstract reasoning, language, introspection, and problem solving.

Role

A Role or a social Role is a set of connected behaviors, rights and obligations as conceptualized by actors in a social situation. It is an expected or free or continously changing behavior and may have a given individual social status or social position. It is vital to both functionalist and interactionist understandings of society. Social Role posits the following about social behavior:

· The division of labor in society takes the form of the interaction among heterogeneous specialized positions, we call Roles.

· Social Roles included appropriate and permitted forms of behavior, guided by social norms, which are commonly known and hence determine the expectations for appropriate behavior in these Roles.

· Roles are occupied by individuals, who are called actors.

· When individuals approve of a social Role (i.e., they consider the Role legitimate and constructive, they will incur costs to conform to Role norms, and will also incur costs to punish those who violate Role norms.

· Changed conditions can render a social Role outdated or illegitimate, in which case social pressures are likely to lead to Role change.

· The anticipation of rewards and punishments, as well as the satisfaction of behaving prosocially, account for why agents conform to Role requirmeets.

Monitoring	To monitor or Monitoring generally means to be aware of the state of a system. Below are specific examples:

· to observe a situation for any changes which may occur over time, using a monitor or measuring device of some sort:

· Baby monitor, medical monitor, Heart rate monitor

· BioMonitoring

· Cure Monitoring for composite materials manufacturing

· Deformation Monitoring

· Election Monitoring

· Mining Monitoring

· Natural hazard Monitoring

· Network Monitoring

· Structural Monitoring

· Website Monitoring

· Futures Monitoring, Media Monitoring service

· to observe the behaviour or communications of individuals or groups

· Monitoring competence at a task.

· Clinical Monitoring for new medical drugs
Monitoring Integration Platform

· Indiktor - Monitoring Integration Platform

·

Telerobotics	Telerobotics is the area of robotics concerned with the control of robots from a distance, chiefly using wireless connections (like Wi-Fi, Bluetooth, the Deep Space Network, and similar), `tethered` connections, teleoperation and telepresence. Teleoperation means `doing work at a distance`, although `work` may mean almost anything.
Examination	A competitive Examination is an Examination where applicants compete for a limited number of positions, as opposed to merely having to reach a certain level to pass.
	A comprehensive Examination is a specific type of exam taken by graduate students, which may determine their eligibility to continue their studies.
	In the UK an Examination is usually supervised by an invigilator.
Cancer	Cancer (medical term: malignant neoplasm) is a class of diseases in which a group of cells display uncontrolled growth, invasion that intrudes upon and destroys adjacent tissues, and sometimes metastasis, or spreading to other locations in the body via lymph or blood. These three malignant properties of cancers differentiate them from benign tumors, which do not invade or metastasize.
	Researchers divide the causes of cancer into two groups: those with an environmental cause and those with a hereditary genetic cause.

Chapter 2. Nursing Models: Normal Science for Nursing Practice,

Clinical Trial	Clinical trials are conducted to allow safety (or more specifically, information about adverse drug reactions and adverse effects of other treatments) and efficacy data to be collected for health interventions (e.g., drugs, diagnostics, devices, therapy protocols). These trials can take place only after satisfactory information has been gathered on the quality of the non-clinical safety, and Health Authority/Ethics Committee approval is granted in the country where the trial is taking place. Depending on the type of product and the stage of its development, investigators enroll healthy volunteers and/or patients into small pilot studies initially, followed by larger scale studies in patients that often compare the new product with the currently prescribed treatment.
Empathy	Empathy is the capacity to recognize and, to some extent, share feelings (such as sadness or happiness) that are being experienced by another semi-sentient being. Someone may need to have a certain amount of empathy before they are able to feel compassion. Etymology The English word is derived from the Greek word ?μπ?θεια (empatheia), "physical affection, passion, partiality" which comes from ?v (en), "in, at" + π?θος (pathos), "passion" or "suffering".
Goal	Goal refers to a method of scoring in many sports. It can also refer to the physical structure or area of the playing surface in which a score is made. The structure of a Goal can vary widely from sport to sport.
Kidney	As distinct from the Western medical concept of Kidneys, this concept from Traditional Chinese Medicine is more a way of describing a set of interrelated parts than an anatomical organ.

Chapter 2. Nursing Models: Normal Science for Nursing Practice,

	To differentiate between western or eastern concepts of organs the first letter is capitalized (Liver, instead of liver, Spleen instead of spleen). Because Traditional Chinese Medicine (TCM) is holistic, each organ cannot be explained fully unless the TCM relationship/homeostasis with the other organs is understood.
Learning	Learning is acquiring new or modifying existing knowledge, behaviors, skills, values, or preferences and may involve synthesizing different types of information. The ability to learn is possessed by humans, animals and some machines. Progress over time tends to follow learning curves.

Self-Awareness	Self-awareness is literally consciousness of one's self. It is related to but not identical with self-consciousness
	
	I think, therefore I am
	
	`...And as I observed that this truth `I think, therefore I am` (Cogito ergo sum) was so certain and of such evidence ...I concluded that I might, without scruple, accept it as the first principle of the Philosophy I was in search.`
	
	`...In the statement `I think, therefore I am` ...I see very clearly that to think it is necessary to be, I concluded that I might take, as a general rule, the principle, that all the things which we very clearly and distinctly conceive are true...`
	
	While reading Descartes, Locke began to relish the great ideas of philosophy and the scientific method. On one occasion, while in a meeting with friends, the question of the `limits of human understanding` arose.

Theory	Originally the word theory is a technical term from Ancient Greek. It is derived from theoria, θεωρ?α, meaning "a looking at, viewing, beholding", and refers to contemplation or speculation, as opposed to action. Theory is especially often contrasted to "practice" a concept that in its original Aristotelian context referred to actions done for their own sake, but can also refer to "technical" actions instrumental to some other aim, such as the making of tools or houses.

Chapter 2. Nursing Models: Normal Science for Nursing Practice,

Womanhood	Womanhood is the period in a female's life after she has transitioned from girlhood, at least physically, having passed the age of menarche. Many cultures have rites of passage to symbolize a woman's coming of age, such as confirmation in some branches of Christianity, bat mitzvah in Judaism, or even just the custom of a special celebration for a certain birthday (generally between 12 and 21). The word woman can be used generally, to mean any female human, or specifically, to mean an adult female human as contrasted with girl.
Self-Care Deficit Nursing Theory	The self-care deficit nursing theory is a grand nursing theory that was developed between 1959 and 2001 by Dorothea Orem. It is also known as the Orem model of nursing. It is particularly used in rehabilitation and primary care settings where the patient is encouraged to be as independent as possible.
Education	Education in the largest sense is any act or experience that has a formative effect on the mind, character or physical ability of an individual. In its technical sense, education is the process by which society deliberately transmits its accumulated knowledge, skills and values from one generation to another. Etymologically, the word education is derived from educare "bring up", which is related to educere "bring out", "bring forth what is within", "bring out potential" and ducere, "to lead".
Adaptation	Adaptation is the process whereby a population becomes better suited to its habitat. This process takes place over many generations, and is one of the basic phenomena of biology. The significance of an Adaptation can only be understood in relation to the total biology of the species.
Customer	A customer buyer, is usually used to refer to a current or potential buyer or user of the products of an individual or organization, called the supplier, seller, or vendor. This is typically through purchasing or renting goods or services. However, in certain contexts, the term customer also includes by extension anyone who uses or experiences the services of another.
Healing	Physiological healing is the restoration of damaged living tissue to normal function. It is the process by which the cells in the body regenerate and repair to reduce the size of a damaged or necrotic area. Healing incorporates both the removal of necrotic tissue (demolition), and the replacement of this tissue.

| Knowledge | Knowledge is defined by the Oxford English Dictionary as (i) expertise, and skills acquired by a person through experience or education; the theoretical or practical understanding of a subject; (ii) what is known in a particular field or in total; facts and information; or (iii) be absolutely certain or sure about something. Philosophical debates in general start with Plato's formulation of knowledge as "justified true belief." There is however no single agreed definition of knowledge presently, nor any prospect of one, and there remain numerous competing theories. Knowledge acquisition involves complex cognitive processes: perception, learning, communication, association and reasoning. |

Chapter 3. Philosophies, Models, and Theories: Critical Thinking Structures,

Nursing	Nursing is a healthcare profession focused on the care of individuals, families, and communities so they may attain, maintain, or recover optimal health and quality of life from conception to death.
	Nurses work in a large variety of specialties where they work independently and as part of a team to assess, plan, implement and evaluate care. Nursing Science is a field of knowledge based on the contributions of nursing scientist through peer reviewed scholarly journals and evidenced-based practice.
Theory	Originally the word theory is a technical term from Ancient Greek. It is derived from theoria, θεωρ? α, meaning "a looking at, viewing, beholding", and refers to contemplation or speculation, as opposed to action. Theory is especially often contrasted to "practice" a concept that in its original Aristotelian context referred to actions done for their own sake, but can also refer to "technical" actions instrumental to some other aim, such as the making of tools or houses.
Theories	[For a more detailed account of theories as expressed in formal language as they are studied in mathematical logic see Theory (mathematical logic.)] The term theory has two broad sets of meanings, one used in the empirical sciences (both natural and social) and the other used in philosophy, mathematics, logic, and across other fields in the humanities. There is considerable difference and even dispute across academic disciplines as to the proper usages of the term. What follows is an attempt to describe how the term is used, not to try to say how it ought to be used.
Paradigm	The word paradigm has been used in science to describe distinct concepts. It comes from Greek "παρ?δειγμα" (paradeigma), "pattern, example, sample" from the verb "παραδε? κνυμι" (paradeiknumi), "exhibit, represent, expose" and that from "παρ?" (para), "beside, by" + "δε?κνυμι" (deiknumi), "to show, to point out".
	The original Greek term παραδε?γματι (paradeigma) was used in Greek texts such as Plato's Timaeus (28A) as the model or the pattern that the Demiurge (god) used to create the cosmos.

Chapter 3. Philosophies, Models, and Theories: Critical Thinking Structures,

Nursing theory	Nursing theory is the term given to the body of knowledge that is used to define or explain various aspects of the profession of nursing.
	Types of nursing theories
	Grand nursing theories
	Grand nursing theories have the broadest scope and present general concepts and propositions. Theories at this level may both reflect and provide insights useful for practice but are not designed for empirical testing.
Orthopedic	Orthopedic surgery or Orthopedics (also spelled orthopaedics) is the branch of surgery concerned with conditions involving the musculoskeletal system. Orthopedic surgeons use both surgical and non-surgical means to treat musculoskeletal trauma, sports injuries, degenerative diseases, infections, tumors, and congenital conditions.
	Nicholas Andry coined the word `orthopaedics`, derived from Greek words for orthos and paideion (`child`), when he published Orthopaedia: or the Art of Correcting and Preventing Deformities in Children in 1741.
Osteoporosis	Osteoporosis is a disease of bone that leads to an increased risk of fracture. In Osteoporosis the bone mineral density (BMD) is reduced, bone microarchitecture is disrupted, and the amount and variety of non-collagenous proteins in bone is altered. Osteoporosis is defined by the World Health Organization (WHO) in women as a bone mineral density 2.5 standard deviations below peak bone mass (20-year-old healthy female average) as measured by DXA; the term `established Osteoporosis` includes the presence of a fragility fracture.
Outcome	In game theory, an outcome is a set of moves or strategies taken by the players, or their payoffs resulting from the actions or strategies taken by all players. The two are complementary in that, given knowledge of the set of strategies of all players, the final state of the game is known, as are any relevant payoffs. In a game where chance or a random event is involved, the outcome is not known from only the set of strategies, but is only realized when the random event(s) are realized.

Chapter 3. Philosophies, Models, and Theories: Critical Thinking Structures,

Notes on Nursing	Notes on Nursing: What it is and What it is Not is a book first published by Florence Nightingale in 1859. A 136-page volume, it was intended to give hints on nursing to those entrusted with the health of others. Florence Nightingale stressed that it was not meant to be a comprehensive guide from which to teach one's self to be a nurse but to help in the practice of treating others.

In her introduction to the 1974 edition, Joan Quixley, then head of the Nightingale School of Nursing, wrote that despite the passage of time since Notes on Nursing was published, "the book astonishes one with its relevance to modern attitudes and skills in nursing, whether this be practised at home by the 'ordinary woman', in hospital or in the community. |
| Health | At the time of the creation of the World Health Organization (WHO), in 1948, Health was defined as being `a state of complete physical, mental, and social well-being and not merely the absence of disease or infirmity`.
This definition invited nations to expand the conceptual framework of their Health systems beyond issues related to the physical condition of individuals and their diseases, and it motivated us to focus our attention on what we now call social determinants of Health. Consequently, WHO challenged political, academic, community, and professional organizations devoted to improving or preserving Health to make the scope of their work explicit, including their rationale for allocating resources. |
| Social | The term Social refers to a characteristic of living organisms (humans in particular, though biologists also apply the term to populations of other animals). It always refers to the interaction of organisms with other organisms and to their collective co-existence, irrespective of whether they are aware of it or not, and irrespective of whether the interaction is voluntary or involuntary.

In the absence of agreement about its meaning, the term `Social` is used in many different senses and regarded as a fuzzy concept, referring among other things to: |

· Attitudes, orientations, or behaviours which take the interests, intentions, or needs of other people into account (in contrast to anti-Social behaviour);has played some role in defining the idea or the principle. For instance terms like Social realism, Social justice, Social constructivism, Social psychology and Social capital imply that there is some Social process involved or considered, a process that is not there in regular, `non-Social`, realism, justice, constructivism, psychology, or capital.

Social Support

Social support is the physical and emotional comfort given to us by our family, friends, co-workers and others. It is knowing that we are part of a community of people who love and care for us, and value and think well of us. Social support is a way of categorizing the rewards of communication in a particular circumstance.

Role

A Role or a social Role is a set of connected behaviors, rights and obligations as conceptualized by actors in a social situation. It is an expected or free or continously changing behavior and may have a given individual social status or social position. It is vital to both functionalist and interactionist understandings of society. Social Role posits the following about social behavior:

· The division of labor in society takes the form of the interaction among heterogeneous specialized positions, we call Roles.

· Social Roles included appropriate and permitted forms of behavior, guided by social norms, which are commonly known and hence determine the expectations for appropriate behavior in these Roles.

· Roles are occupied by individuals, who are called actors.

· When individuals approve of a social Role (i.e., they consider the Role legitimate and constructive, they will incur costs to conform to Role norms, and will also incur costs to punish those who violate Role norms.

· Changed conditions can render a social Role outdated or illegitimate, in which case social pressures are likely to lead to Role change.

· The anticipation of rewards and punishments, as well as the satisfaction of behaving prosocially, account for why agents conform to Role requirmeets.

Telerobotics

Telerobotics is the area of robotics concerned with the control of robots from a distance, chiefly using wireless connections (like Wi-Fi, Bluetooth, the Deep Space Network, and similar), `tethered` connections, teleoperation and telepresence.

Chapter 3. Philosophies, Models, and Theories: Critical Thinking Structures,

	Teleoperation means `doing work at a distance`, although `work` may mean almost anything.
Empathy	Empathy is the capacity to recognize and, to some extent, share feelings (such as sadness or happiness) that are being experienced by another semi-sentient being. Someone may need to have a certain amount of empathy before they are able to feel compassion.
	Etymology
	The English word is derived from the Greek word ?μπ?θεια (empatheia), "physical affection, passion, partiality" which comes from ?v (en), "in, at" + π?θος (pathos), "passion" or "suffering".
Cancer	Cancer (medical term: malignant neoplasm) is a class of diseases in which a group of cells display uncontrolled growth, invasion that intrudes upon and destroys adjacent tissues, and sometimes metastasis, or spreading to other locations in the body via lymph or blood. These three malignant properties of cancers differentiate them from benign tumors, which do not invade or metastasize.
	Researchers divide the causes of cancer into two groups: those with an environmental cause and those with a hereditary genetic cause.
Clinical Trial	Clinical trials are conducted to allow safety (or more specifically, information about adverse drug reactions and adverse effects of other treatments) and efficacy data to be collected for health interventions (e.g., drugs, diagnostics, devices, therapy protocols). These trials can take place only after satisfactory information has been gathered on the quality of the non-clinical safety, and Health Authority/Ethics Committee approval is granted in the country where the trial is taking place.
	Depending on the type of product and the stage of its development, investigators enroll healthy volunteers and/or patients into small pilot studies initially, followed by larger scale studies in patients that often compare the new product with the currently prescribed treatment.

Chapter 3. Philosophies, Models, and Theories: Critical Thinking Structures,

Energy	Mental or psychic energy is the concept of a principle of activity powering the operation of the mind or psyche. Many modern psychologists or neuroscientists would equate it with increased metabolism in neurons of the brain.
	Philosophical accounts
	The idea harks back to Aristotle's conception of actus et potentia.
Goal	Goal refers to a method of scoring in many sports. It can also refer to the physical structure or area of the playing surface in which a score is made.
	The structure of a Goal can vary widely from sport to sport.
Learning	Learning is acquiring new or modifying existing knowledge, behaviors, skills, values, or preferences and may involve synthesizing different types of information. The ability to learn is possessed by humans, animals and some machines. Progress over time tends to follow learning curves.
Self-Awareness	Self-awareness is literally consciousness of one's self. It is related to but not identical with self-consciousness
	I think,therefore I am
	`...And as I observed that this truth `I think, therefore I am` (Cogito ergo sum) was so certain and of such evidence ...I concluded that I might, without scruple, accept it as the first principle of the Philosophy I was in search.`
	`...In the statement `I think, therefore I am` ...I see very clearly that to think it is necessary to be, I concluded that I might take, as a general rule, the principle, that all the things which we very clearly and distinctly conceive are true...`

Chapter 3. Philosophies, Models, and Theories: Critical Thinking Structures,

	While reading Descartes, Locke began to relish the great ideas of philosophy and the scientific method. On one occasion, while in a meeting with friends, the question of the `limits of human understanding` arose.
Womanhood	Womanhood is the period in a female`s life after she has transitioned from girlhood, at least physically, having passed the age of menarche. Many cultures have rites of passage to symbolize a woman`s coming of age, such as confirmation in some branches of Christianity, bat mitzvah in Judaism, or even just the custom of a special celebration for a certain birthday (generally between 12 and 21). The word woman can be used generally, to mean any female human, or specifically, to mean an adult female human as contrasted with girl.
Customer	A customer buyer, is usually used to refer to a current or potential buyer or user of the products of an individual or organization, called the supplier, seller, or vendor. This is typically through purchasing or renting goods or services. However, in certain contexts, the term customer also includes by extension anyone who uses or experiences the services of another.
Health Promotion	Health promotion has been defined by the World Health Organization`s 2005 Bangkok Charter for Health promotion in a Globalized World as `the process of enabling people to increase control over their health and its determinants, and thereby improve their health`. The primary means of Health promotion occur through developing healthy public policy that addresses the prerequisities of health such as income, housing, food security, employment, and quality working conditions. There is a tendency among public health officials and governments -- and this is especially the case in liberal nations such as Canada and the USA -- to reduce Health promotion to health education and social marketing focused on changing behavioral risk factors.
Health care	Health care , refers to the treatment and management of illness, and the preservation of health through services offered by the medical, dental, complementary and alternative medicine, pharmaceutical, clinical laboratory sciences , nursing, and allied health professions. Health care embraces all the goods and services designed to promote health, including `preventive, curative and palliative interventions, whether directed to individuals or to populations`. Before the term Health care became popular, English-speakers referred to medicine or to the health sector and spoke of the treatment and prevention of illness and disease.
Intention	An agent's intention in performing an action is his or her specific purpose in doing so, the end or goal that is aimed at, or intended to accomplish. Whether an action is successful or unsuccessful depends at least on whether the intended result was brought about. Other consequences of someone`s acting are called unintentional.

Pressure	Example reading: $1\ Pa = 1\ N/m^2 = 10^{-5}\ bar = 10.197 \times 10^{-6}\ at = 9.8692 \times 10^{-6}\ atm$, etc.
	As an example of varying Pressures, a finger can be pressed against a wall without making any lasting impression; however, the same finger pushing a thumbtack can easily damage the wall. Although the force applied to the surface is the same, the thumbtack applies more Pressure because the point concentrates that force into a smaller area.
Preterm	In humans, preterm birth refers to the birth of a baby of less than 37 weeks gestational age. Premature birth, commonly used as a synonym f birth, refers to the birth of a premature infant. The child may commonly be referred to throughout their life as being born a `preemie` or `preemie baby`.
Prevention	Prevention refers to:
	· Preventive medicine
	· Hazard Prevention, the process of risk study and elimination and mitigation in emergency management
	· Risk Prevention
	· Risk management
	· Preventive maintenance
	· Crime Prevention
	· Prevention, an album by Scottish band De Rosa
	· Prevention a magazine about health in the United States
	· Prevent (company), a textile company from Slovenia

Chapter 3. Philosophies, Models, and Theories: Critical Thinking Structures,

Therapeutic	Therapy is the attempted remediation of a health problem, usually following a diagnosis. In the medical field, it is synonymous with the word `treatment`.
	A therapeutic effect is a consequence of a particular treatment which is judged to be desirable and beneficial.
Monitoring	To monitor or Monitoring generally means to be aware of the state of a system. Below are specific examples:
	· to observe a situation for any changes which may occur over time, using a monitor or measuring device of some sort:
	· Baby monitor, medical monitor, Heart rate monitor
	· BioMonitoring
	· Cure Monitoring for composite materials manufacturing
	· Deformation Monitoring
	· Election Monitoring
	· Mining Monitoring
	· Natural hazard Monitoring
	· Network Monitoring
	· Structural Monitoring
	· Website Monitoring
	· Futures Monitoring, Media Monitoring service
	· to observe the behaviour or communications of individuals or groups

· Monitoring competence at a task.

· Clinical Monitoring for new medical drugs
Monitoring Integration Platform

· Indiktor - Monitoring Integration Platform

·

Self-Care Deficit Nursing Theory	The self-care deficit nursing theory is a grand nursing theory that was developed between 1959 and 2001 by Dorothea Orem. It is also known as the Orem model of nursing. It is particularly used in rehabilitation and primary care settings where the patient is encouraged to be as independent as possible.
Heart	The Heart is one of the zàng organs stipulated by Traditional Chinese Medicine (TCM). It is a functionally defined entity and not equivalent to the anatomical organ of the same name. In the context of the zang-fu concept As a zàng, the Heart is considered to be a yin organ.
Humans	Humans commonly refers to the species Homo sapiens , the only extant member of the Homo genus of bipedal primates in Hominidae, the great ape family. However, in some cases the term is used to refer to any member of the genus Homo. Humans have a highly developed brain, capable of abstract reasoning, language, introspection, and problem solving.

Openness	Openness is a very general philosophical position from which some individuals and organizations operate, often highlighted by a decision-making process recognizing communal management by distributed stakeholders (users/producers/contributors) rather than a centralized authority (owners, experts, boards of directors, etc).
	Openness could be a synonym of :
	.
Science of Unitary Human Beings	The science of unitary human beings is a grand nursing theory developed by Martha E. Rogers. The details of the theory are included in her book, An Introduction to the Theoretical Basis of Nursing.
	Overview
	According to Rogers, Nursing is both a science and an art.
Education	Education in the largest sense is any act or experience that has a formative effect on the mind, character or physical ability of an individual. In its technical sense, education is the process by which society deliberately transmits its accumulated knowledge, skills and values from one generation to another.
	Etymologically, the word education is derived from educare "bring up", which is related to educere "bring out", "bring forth what is within", "bring out potential" and ducere, "to lead".
Abuse	Abuse is defined as:
	Abuse of information typically involves a breach of confidence or plagiarism.

	Abuse of power, in the form of 'malfeasance in office' or 'official misconduct', is the commission of an unlawful act, done in an official capacity, which affects the performance of official duties. Malfeasance in office is often grounds for a for cause removal of an elected official by statute or recall election.
Adaptation	Adaptation is the process whereby a population becomes better suited to its habitat. This process takes place over many generations, and is one of the basic phenomena of biology. The significance of an Adaptation can only be understood in relation to the total biology of the species.
Knowledge	Knowledge is defined by the Oxford English Dictionary as (i) expertise, and skills acquired by a person through experience or education; the theoretical or practical understanding of a subject; (ii) what is known in a particular field or in total; facts and information; or (iii) be absolutely certain or sure about something. Philosophical debates in general start with Plato's formulation of knowledge as "justified true belief." There is however no single agreed definition of knowledge presently, nor any prospect of one, and there remain numerous competing theories. Knowledge acquisition involves complex cognitive processes: perception, learning, communication, association and reasoning.
Nursing Process	The nursing process is a process by which nurses deliver care to individuals, families, and/or communities and is supported by nursing theories. The nursing process was originally an adapted form of problem-solving and is classified as a deductive theory. Phases of the nursing process The nursing process is a client-centered, goal-oriented method of caring that provides a framework to nursing care.
Best practice	Best practice is a coined expression or neologism used to designate a technique, method, process, activity, incentive, or reward which is regarded as more effective at delivering a particular outcome than any other technique, method, process, etc. when applied to a particular condition or circumstance. The idea is that with proper processes, checks, and testing, a desired outcome can be delivered with fewer problems and unforeseen complications.

Chapter 3. Philosophies, Models, and Theories: Critical Thinking Structures,

Nursing practice	Nursing practice is the actual provision of nursing care. In providing care, nurses are implementing the nursing care plan which is based on the client's initial assessment. This is based around a specific nursing theory which will be selected as appropriate for the care setting.
Selection	In the context of evolution, certain traits or alleles of genes segregating within a population may be subject to selection. Under selection, individuals with advantageous or "adaptive" traits tend to be more successful than their peers reproductively--meaning they contribute more offspring to the succeeding generation than others do. When these traits have a genetic basis, selection can increase the prevalence of those traits, because offspring will inherit those traits from their parents.
Commission on Collegiate Nursing Education	The Commission on Collegiate Nursing Education is an autonomous nursing education accrediting agency that contributes to the improvement of the public's health. The CCNE is recognized by the U.S. Secretary of Education as a national accreditation agency. CCNE accreditation is a voluntary, self-regulatory process, and the organization encourages and supports nursing education programs to perform self-assessments to grow and improve their collegiate professional education.
Healing	Physiological healing is the restoration of damaged living tissue to normal function. It is the process by which the cells in the body regenerate and repair to reduce the size of a damaged or necrotic area. Healing incorporates both the removal of necrotic tissue (demolition), and the replacement of this tissue.

Chapter 4. Philosophies, Models, and Theories: Moral Obligations,

Ethics	Ethics is a branch of philosophy that addresses questions about morality--that is, concepts such as good and evil, right and wrong, virtue and vice, justice, etc. Major branches of ethics include: • Meta-ethics, about the theoretical meaning and reference of moral propositions and how their truth-values (if any) may be determined; • Normative ethics, about the practical means of determining a moral course of action; • Applied ethics, about how moral outcomes can be achieved in specific situations; • Moral psychology, about how moral capacity or moral agency develops and what its nature is; • Descriptive ethics, about what moral values people actually abide by. Within each of these branches are many different schools of thought and still further sub-fields of study. Meta-ethics Meta-ethics is the branch of ethics that seeks to understand the nature of ethical properties, and ethical statements, attitudes, and judgments.
Nursing	Nursing is a healthcare profession focused on the care of individuals, families, and communities so they may attain, maintain, or recover optimal health and quality of life from conception to death. Nurses work in a large variety of specialties where they work independently and as part of a team to assess, plan, implement and evaluate care. Nursing Science is a field of knowledge based on the contributions of nursing scientist through peer reviewed scholarly journals and evidenced-based practice.

Chapter 4. Philosophies, Models, and Theories: Moral Obligations,

Knowledge	Knowledge is defined by the Oxford English Dictionary as (i) expertise, and skills acquired by a person through experience or education; the theoretical or practical understanding of a subject; (ii) what is known in a particular field or in total; facts and information; or (iii) be absolutely certain or sure about something. Philosophical debates in general start with Plato's formulation of knowledge as "justified true belief." There is however no single agreed definition of knowledge presently, nor any prospect of one, and there remain numerous competing theories. Knowledge acquisition involves complex cognitive processes: perception, learning, communication, association and reasoning.
String searching algorithms	String searching algorithms are an important class of string algorithms that try to find a place where one or several strings are found within a larger string or text. Let Σ be an alphabet (finite set). Formally, both the pattern and searched text are concatenations of elements of Σ.
Scope	Scope is a London-based charity, which operates in England and Wales, focusing on people with cerebral palsy particularly, and disabled people in general. Its aim is that disabled people achieve equality. Scope was founded on 9 October 1952 by Ian Dawson-Shepherd, Eric Hodgson, Alex Moira and a social worker, Jean Garwood.
Nursing practice	Nursing practice is the actual provision of nursing care. In providing care, nurses are implementing the nursing care plan which is based on the client's initial assessment. This is based around a specific nursing theory which will be selected as appropriate for the care setting.
Nursing theory	Nursing theory is the term given to the body of knowledge that is used to define or explain various aspects of the profession of nursing. Types of nursing theories Grand nursing theories

Chapter 4. Philosophies, Models, and Theories: Moral Obligations,

Grand nursing theories have the broadest scope and present general concepts and propositions. Theories at this level may both reflect and provide insights useful for practice but are not designed for empirical testing.

American Nurses Association	The American Nurses Association is a professional organization to advance and protect the profession of nursing. It started in 1896 as the Nurses Associated Alumnae and was renamed the American Nurses Association in 1911. It is based in Silver Spring, Maryland and Rebecca M. Patton, MSN, RN, CNOR, is the current President.

The Association is a professional organization representing registered nurses (RNs) in the United States through its 54 constituent member associations. |
| Nurse | A Nurse is a healthcare professional who, in collaboration with other members of a health care team, is responsible for: treatment, safety, and recovery of acutely or chronically ill individuals; health promotion and maintenance within families, communities and populations; and, treatment of life-threatening emergencies in a wide range of health care settings. Nurses perform a wide range of clinical and non-clinical functions necessary to the delivery of health care, and may also be involved in medical and nursing research.

Both Nursing roles and education were first defined by Florence Nightingale, following her experiences caring for the wounded in the Crimean War. |
| Nurses | · EMTs and Paramedics work closely with emergency and critical care Nurses to stabilize life-threatening trauma and medical emergencies and to provide a seamless transfer of care from incoming ambulances to awaiting medical/surgical teams.

· Technicians: , certified medication aides in the US, are trained to administer medications in a long-term care setting. There are also phlebotomy technicians, who perform venipuncture; surgical technologist (US), and technicians trained to operate most kinds of diagnostic and laboratory equipment, such as X-ray machines, electrocardiographs, and so forth. |

Chapter 4. Philosophies, Models, and Theories: Moral Obligations,

Statements	Statements is an international medical symposium, which takes place every two years since 2004. Researcher, medical scientists and physicians on the field of head and neck cancer meet to discuss recent scientific and clinical findings.
	The first event took place in Frankfurt am Main, Germany in 2004.
	Concept
	"Statements on head and neck cancer" was founded in 2004 by the non-profit society "Verein Prävention und Therapie e.V.".
Theory	Originally the word theory is a technical term from Ancient Greek. It is derived from theoria, θεωρ?α, meaning "a looking at, viewing, beholding", and refers to contemplation or speculation, as opposed to action. Theory is especially often contrasted to "practice" a concept that in its original Aristotelian context referred to actions done for their own sake, but can also refer to "technical" actions instrumental to some other aim, such as the making of tools or houses.
Goal	Goal refers to a method of scoring in many sports. It can also refer to the physical structure or area of the playing surface in which a score is made.
	The structure of a Goal can vary widely from sport to sport.
Health	At the time of the creation of the World Health Organization (WHO), in 1948, Health was defined as being `a state of complete physical, mental, and social well-being and not merely the absence of disease or infirmity`.
This definition invited nations to expand the conceptual framework of their Health systems beyond issues related to the physical condition of individuals and their diseases, and it motivated us to focus our attention on what we now call social determinants of Health. Consequently, WHO challenged political, academic, community, and professional organizations devoted to improving or preserving Health to make the scope of their work explicit, including their rationale for allocating resources.

Chapter 4. Philosophies, Models, and Theories: Moral Obligations,

Concept	A concept is a cognitive unit of meaning--an abstract idea or a mental symbol sometimes defined as a "unit of knowledge," built from other units which act as a concept's characteristics. A concept is typically associated with a corresponding representation in a language or symbology such as a single meaning of a term. There are prevailing theories in contemporary philosophy which attempt to explain the nature of concepts.
House	A House is generally a shelter, building or structure that is a dwelling or place for habitation by human beings. The term includes many kinds of dwellings ranging from rudimentary huts of nomadic tribes to high-rise apartment buildings. In some contexts, `House` may mean the same as dwelling, residence, home, abode, lodging, accommodation, or housing, among other meanings.
Selection	In the context of evolution, certain traits or alleles of genes segregating within a population may be subject to selection. Under selection, individuals with advantageous or "adaptive" traits tend to be more successful than their peers reproductively--meaning they contribute more offspring to the succeeding generation than others do. When these traits have a genetic basis, selection can increase the prevalence of those traits, because offspring will inherit those traits from their parents.
Adaptation	Adaptation is the process whereby a population becomes better suited to its habitat. This process takes place over many generations, and is one of the basic phenomena of biology. The significance of an Adaptation can only be understood in relation to the total biology of the species.
Education	Education in the largest sense is any act or experience that has a formative effect on the mind, character or physical ability of an individual. In its technical sense, education is the process by which society deliberately transmits its accumulated knowledge, skills and values from one generation to another.

Etymologically, the word education is derived from educare "bring up", which is related to educere "bring out", "bring forth what is within", "bring out potential" and ducere, "to lead".

Self-Care Deficit Nursing Theory	The self-care deficit nursing theory is a grand nursing theory that was developed between 1959 and 2001 by Dorothea Orem. It is also known as the Orem model of nursing. It is particularly used in rehabilitation and primary care settings where the patient is encouraged to be as independent as possible.
Nursing Process	The nursing process is a process by which nurses deliver care to individuals, families, and/or communities and is supported by nursing theories. The nursing process was originally an adapted form of problem-solving and is classified as a deductive theory.

Phases of the nursing process

The nursing process is a client-centered, goal-oriented method of caring that provides a framework to nursing care. |

Chapter 5. Nightingale`s Philosophy in Nursing Practice,

NICU	A neonatal intensive care unit, usually shortened NICU and also called a newborn intensive care unit, intensive care nursery (ICN), and special care baby unit , or a humidicrib, is a unit of a hospital specializing in the care of ill or premature newborn infants. The NICU is distinct from a special care nursery in providing a high level of intensive care to premature infants while the SCN provides specialized care for infants with less severe medical problems.
	NICUs were developed in the 1950s and 1960s by pediatricians to provide better temperature support, isolation from infection risk, specialized feeding, and greater access to specialized equipment and resources.
Nursing	Nursing is a healthcare profession focused on the care of individuals, families, and communities so they may attain, maintain, or recover optimal health and quality of life from conception to death.
	Nurses work in a large variety of specialties where they work independently and as part of a team to assess, plan, implement and evaluate care. Nursing Science is a field of knowledge based on the contributions of nursing scientist through peer reviewed scholarly journals and evidenced-based practice.
Humans	Humans commonly refers to the species Homo sapiens , the only extant member of the Homo genus of bipedal primates in Hominidae, the great ape family. However, in some cases the term is used to refer to any member of the genus Homo.
	Humans have a highly developed brain, capable of abstract reasoning, language, introspection, and problem solving.
Notes on Nursing	Notes on Nursing: What it is and What it is Not is a book first published by Florence Nightingale in 1859. A 136-page volume, it was intended to give hints on nursing to those entrusted with the health of others. Florence Nightingale stressed that it was not meant to be a comprehensive guide from which to teach one's self to be a nurse but to help in the practice of treating others.

Chapter 5. Nightingale's Philosophy in Nursing Practice,

In her introduction to the 1974 edition, Joan Quixley, then head of the Nightingale School of Nursing, wrote that despite the passage of time since Notes on Nursing was published, "the book astonishes one with its relevance to modern attitudes and skills in nursing, whether this be practised at home by the 'ordinary woman', in hospital or in the community.

Customer	A customer buyer, is usually used to refer to a current or potential buyer or user of the products of an individual or organization, called the supplier, seller, or vendor. This is typically through purchasing or renting goods or services. However, in certain contexts, the term customer also includes by extension anyone who uses or experiences the services of another.
Healing	Physiological healing is the restoration of damaged living tissue to normal function. It is the process by which the cells in the body regenerate and repair to reduce the size of a damaged or necrotic area. Healing incorporates both the removal of necrotic tissue (demolition), and the replacement of this tissue.
Health	At the time of the creation of the World Health Organization (WHO), in 1948, Health was defined as being `a state of complete physical, mental, and social well-being and not merely the absence of disease or infirmity`. This definition invited nations to expand the conceptual framework of their Health systems beyond issues related to the physical condition of individuals and their diseases, and it motivated us to focus our attention on what we now call social determinants of Health. Consequently, WHO challenged political, academic, community, and professional organizations devoted to improving or preserving Health to make the scope of their work explicit, including their rationale for allocating resources.
Midwifery	A Certified Professional Midwife (CPM) is a knowledgeable, skilled and professional independent Midwifery practitioner who has met the standards for certification set by the North American Registry of Midwives (NARM) and is qualified to provide the midwives model of care. The CPM is the only US credential that requires knowledge about and experience in out-of-hospital settings. At present, there are approximately 900 CPMs practicing in the US. A Licensed Midwife is a midwife who is licensed to practice in a particular state.
Theory	Originally the word theory is a technical term from Ancient Greek. It is derived from theoria, θεωρ? α, meaning "a looking at, viewing, beholding", and refers to contemplation or speculation, as opposed to action. Theory is especially often contrasted to "practice" a concept that in its original Aristotelian context referred to actions done for their own sake, but can also refer to "technical" actions instrumental to some other aim, such as the making of tools or houses.

Chapter 5. Nightingale`s Philosophy in Nursing Practice,

Restrictive	In semantics, a modifier is said to be restrictive if it restricts the reference of its head. For example, in `the red car is fancier than the blue one`, red and blue are restrictive, because they restrict which cars car and one are referring to. (`The car is fancier than the one` would make little sense.)
Assessment	Educational Assessment is the process of documenting, usually in measurable terms, knowledge, skills, attitudes and beliefs. Assessment can focus on the individual learner, the learning community (class, workshop, or other organized group of learners), the institution, or the educational system as a whole. According to the Academic Exchange Quarterly: 'Studies of a theoretical or empirical nature addressing the Assessment of learner aptitude and preparation, motivation and learning styles, learning outcomes in achievement and satisfaction in different educational contexts are all welcome, as are studies addressing issues of measurable standards and benchmarks'.
Nursing Assessment	Nursing assessment is the gathering of information about a patient`s physiological, psychological, sociological, and spiritual status.  Assessment is the first stage of the nursing process in which the nurse should carry out a complete and holistic nursing assessment of every patient`s needs, regardless of the reason for the encounter. Usually, an assessment framework, based on a nursing model is used.
Case study	A case study is a research method common in social science. It is based on an in-depth investigation of a single individual, group, or event. Case studies may be descriptive or explanatory.
Diagnosis	Diagnosis is the identification of the nature and cause of anything. Diagnosis is used in many different disciplines with variations in the use of logics, analytics, and experience to determine the cause and effect relationships. In systems engineering and computer science, diagnosis is typically used to determine the causes of symptoms, mitigations for problems, and solutions to issues.
Nutrition	Nutrition is the provision, to cells and organisms, of the materials necessary (in the form of food) to support life. Many common health problems can be prevented or alleviated with a healthy diet. Overview

Chapter 5. Nightingale's Philosophy in Nursing Practice,

	Nutrition science investigates the metabolic and physiological responses of the body to diet.
Hospice	Hospice is a type of care and a philosophy of care that focuses on the palliation of a terminally ill patient's symptoms. These symptoms can be physical, emotional, spiritual or social in nature. The concept of hospice has been evolving since the 11th century.
House	A House is generally a shelter, building or structure that is a dwelling or place for habitation by human beings. The term includes many kinds of dwellings ranging from rudimentary huts of nomadic tribes to high-rise apartment buildings. In some contexts, `House` may mean the same as dwelling, residence, home, abode, lodging, accommodation, or housing, among other meanings.
Chronic	In medicine, a chronic disease is a disease that is long-lasting or recurrent. The term chronic describes the course of the disease, or its rate of onset and development. A chronic course is distinguished from a recurrent course; recurrent diseases relapse repeatedly, with periods of remission in between.
Ventilation	Ventilation is the intentional movement of air from outside a building to the inside. It is the V in HVAC. With clothes dryers, and combustion equipment such as water heaters, boilers, fireplaces, and wood stoves, their exhausts are often called vents or flues -- this should not be confused with Ventilation. The vents or flues carry the products of combustion which have to be expelled from the building in a way which does not cause harm to the occupants of the building.

Chapter 6. Watson`s Philosophy in Nursing Practice,

Burn	A burn is a type of injury to flesh caused by heat, electricity, chemicals, light, radiation or friction. Most burns only affect the skin (epidermal tissue and dermis). Rarely, deeper tissues, such as muscle, bone, and blood vessels can also be injured.
Cancer	Cancer (medical term: malignant neoplasm) is a class of diseases in which a group of cells display uncontrolled growth, invasion that intrudes upon and destroys adjacent tissues, and sometimes metastasis, or spreading to other locations in the body via lymph or blood. These three malignant properties of cancers differentiate them from benign tumors, which do not invade or metastasize.
	Researchers divide the causes of cancer into two groups: those with an environmental cause and those with a hereditary genetic cause.
Caregiver	Carer (UK, NZ, Australian usage) and Caregiver are words normally used to refer to unpaid relatives or friends who support people with disabilities. The words may be prefixed with `family` `spousal`, `child` to distinguish between different care situations. The general term dependent/dependant care is also used for the service provided.
Humans	Humans commonly refers to the species Homo sapiens , the only extant member of the Homo genus of bipedal primates in Hominidae, the great ape family. However, in some cases the term is used to refer to any member of the genus Homo.
	Humans have a highly developed brain, capable of abstract reasoning, language, introspection, and problem solving.
Science of Unitary Human Beings	The science of unitary human beings is a grand nursing theory developed by Martha E. Rogers. The details of the theory are included in her book, An Introduction to the Theoretical Basis of Nursing.

Overview

According to Rogers, Nursing is both a science and an art. |

Chapter 6. Watson's Philosophy in Nursing Practice,

Management	Management in all business and organizational activities is the act of getting people together to accomplish desired goals and objectives using available resources efficiently and effectively. Management comprises planning, organizing, staffing, leading or directing, and controlling an organization (a group of one or more people or entities) or effort for the purpose of accomplishing a goal. Resourcing encompasses the deployment and manipulation of human resources, financial resources, technological resources, and natural resources.
Nursing	Nursing is a healthcare profession focused on the care of individuals, families, and communities so they may attain, maintain, or recover optimal health and quality of life from conception to death.
	Nurses work in a large variety of specialties where they work independently and as part of a team to assess, plan, implement and evaluate care. Nursing Science is a field of knowledge based on the contributions of nursing scientist through peer reviewed scholarly journals and evidenced-based practice.
Process and Reality	In philosophy, especially metaphysics, the book Process and Reality by Alfred North Whitehead sets out its author's philosophy of organism published in 1929, is a revision of the Gifford Lectures he gave in 1927-28. Process philosophy lays the groundwork for a paradigm of subjectivity, which Whitehead calls a `completed metaphysical language.` (p.
Faith	Faith is the confident belief or trust in the truth or trustworthiness of a person, concept or thing. The English word is thought to date from 1200-50, from the Latin fidem or fidēs, meaning trust, derived from the verb fῡdere, to trust.
	The term is employed in a religious or theological context to refer to a confident belief in a transcendent reality, a religious teacher, a set of scriptures, teachings or a Supreme Being.
Theory	Originally the word theory is a technical term from Ancient Greek. It is derived from theoria, θεωρ?α, meaning "a looking at, viewing, beholding", and refers to contemplation or speculation, as opposed to action. Theory is especially often contrasted to "practice" a concept that in its original Aristotelian context referred to actions done for their own sake, but can also refer to "technical" actions instrumental to some other aim, such as the making of tools or houses.

Chapter 6. Watson's Philosophy in Nursing Practice,

Healing	Physiological healing is the restoration of damaged living tissue to normal function. It is the process by which the cells in the body regenerate and repair to reduce the size of a damaged or necrotic area. Healing incorporates both the removal of necrotic tissue (demolition), and the replacement of this tissue.
Customer	A customer buyer, is usually used to refer to a current or potential buyer or user of the products of an individual or organization, called the supplier, seller, or vendor. This is typically through purchasing or renting goods or services. However, in certain contexts, the term customer also includes by extension anyone who uses or experiences the services of another.
Experience	Experience as a general concept comprises knowledge of or skill in or observation of some thing or some event gained through involvement in or exposure to that thing or event. The history of the word experience aligns it closely with the concept of experiment. The concept of experience generally refers to know-how or procedural knowledge, rather than propositional knowledge: on-the-job training rather than book-learning.
Transpersonal	The term Transpersonal is often used to refer to psychological categories that transcend the normal features of ordinary ego-functioning. That is, stages of psychological growth, or stages of consciousness, that move beyond the rational and precede the mystical. The term is highly associated with the work of Abraham Maslow and his understanding of `peak experiences`, and was first adapted by the human potential movement in the 1960s.
Interaction	Interaction is a kind of action that occurs as two or more objects have an effect upon one another. The idea of a two-way effect is essential in the concept of interaction, as opposed to a one-way causal effect. A closely related term is interconnectivity, which deals with the interactions of interactions within systems: combinations of many simple interactions can lead to surprising emergent phenomena.
Knowledge	Knowledge is defined by the Oxford English Dictionary as (i) expertise, and skills acquired by a person through experience or education; the theoretical or practical understanding of a subject; (ii) what is known in a particular field or in total; facts and information; or (iii) be absolutely certain or sure about something. Philosophical debates in general start with Plato's formulation of knowledge as "justified true belief." There is however no single agreed definition of knowledge presently, nor any prospect of one, and there remain numerous competing theories. Knowledge acquisition involves complex cognitive processes: perception, learning, communication, association and reasoning.

Chapter 6. Watson`s Philosophy in Nursing Practice,

Nursing theory	Nursing theory is the term given to the body of knowledge that is used to define or explain various aspects of the profession of nursing. Types of nursing theories Grand nursing theories Grand nursing theories have the broadest scope and present general concepts and propositions. Theories at this level may both reflect and provide insights useful for practice but are not designed for empirical testing.
Spirit	The English word `Spirit` has many differing meanings and connotations, but commonly refers to a supernatural being or essence -- transcendent and therefore metaphysical in its nature: the Concise Oxford Dictionary defines it as `the non-physical part of a person`. For many people, however, Spirit, like soul, forms a natural part of a being: such people may identify Spirit with mind, or with consciousness, or with the brain. The English word `Spirit` comes from the Latin Spiritus, meaning `breath` , but also `soul, courage, vigor`, ultimately from a PIE root *(s)peis- (to blow).
Cardiac	The heart is a muscular organ found in all vertebrates that is responsible for pumping blood throughout the blood vessels by repeated, rhythmic contractions. The term cardiac means 'related to the heart' and comes from the Greek καρδιî¬, kardia, for 'heart.' The vertebrate heart is composed of cardiac muscle, which is an involuntary striated muscle tissue found only within this organ. The average human heart, beating at 72 beats per minute, will beat approximately 2.5 billion times during an average 66 year lifespan.
Verb	VERB is a physical activity program of the Center for Disease Control, also Prevention of the United States Government. It includes print, online, and television advertising. Verb is a program that helps
Disease	A disease is an abnormal condition affecting the body of an organism. It is often construed to be a medical condition associated with specific symptoms and signs. It may be caused by external factors, such as infectious disease, or it may be caused by internal dysfunctions, such as autoimmune diseases.

Chapter 6. Watson`s Philosophy in Nursing Practice,

Health	At the time of the creation of the World Health Organization (WHO), in 1948, Health was defined as being `a state of complete physical, mental, and social well-being and not merely the absence of disease or infirmity`. This definition invited nations to expand the conceptual framework of their Health systems beyond issues related to the physical condition of individuals and their diseases, and it motivated us to focus our attention on what we now call social determinants of Health. Consequently, WHO challenged political, academic, community, and professional organizations devoted to improving or preserving Health to make the scope of their work explicit, including their rationale for allocating resources.
Illness	Illness is a state of poor health. Illness is sometimes considered another word for disease. Others maintain that fine distinctions exist.
Case study	A case study is a research method common in social science. It is based on an in-depth investigation of a single individual, group, or event. Case studies may be descriptive or explanatory.

Chapter 7. Benner`s Philosophy in Nursing Practice,

Assessment	Educational Assessment is the process of documenting, usually in measurable terms, knowledge, skills, attitudes and beliefs. Assessment can focus on the individual learner, the learning community (class, workshop, or other organized group of learners), the institution, or the educational system as a whole. According to the Academic Exchange Quarterly: 'Studies of a theoretical or empirical nature addressing the Assessment of learner aptitude and preparation, motivation and learning styles, learning outcomes in achievement and satisfaction in different educational contexts are all welcome, as are studies addressing issues of measurable standards and benchmarks'.
Consensus	Medical consensus is a public statement on a particular aspect of medical knowledge available at the time it was written, and that is generally agreed upon as the evidence-based, state-of-the-art (or state-of-science) knowledge by a representative group of experts in that area. Its main objective is to counsel physicians on the best possible and acceptable way to diagnose and treat certain diseases or how to address a particular decision-making area. Therefore, it can be considered an authoritative, community-based consensus decision-making and publication process.
Nursing	Nursing is a healthcare profession focused on the care of individuals, families, and communities so they may attain, maintain, or recover optimal health and quality of life from conception to death. Nurses work in a large variety of specialties where they work independently and as part of a team to assess, plan, implement and evaluate care. Nursing Science is a field of knowledge based on the contributions of nursing scientist through peer reviewed scholarly journals and evidenced-based practice.
Nursing Practice	Nursing practice is the actual provision of nursing care. In providing care, nurses are implementing the nursing care plan which is based on the client`s initial assessment. This is based around a specific nursing theory which will be selected as appropriate for the care setting.
Cardiac	The heart is a muscular organ found in all vertebrates that is responsible for pumping blood throughout the blood vessels by repeated, rhythmic contractions. The term cardiac means 'related to the heart' and comes from the Greek καρδιἠ, kardia, for 'heart.'

Chapter 7. Benner`s Philosophy in Nursing Practice,

The vertebrate heart is composed of cardiac muscle, which is an involuntary striated muscle tissue found only within this organ. The average human heart, beating at 72 beats per minute, will beat approximately 2.5 billion times during an average 66 year lifespan.

Ethics

Ethics is a branch of philosophy that addresses questions about morality--that is, concepts such as good and evil, right and wrong, virtue and vice, justice, etc.

Major branches of ethics include:

- Meta-ethics, about the theoretical meaning and reference of moral propositions and how their truth-values (if any) may be determined;
- Normative ethics, about the practical means of determining a moral course of action;
- Applied ethics, about how moral outcomes can be achieved in specific situations;
- Moral psychology, about how moral capacity or moral agency develops and what its nature is;
- Descriptive ethics, about what moral values people actually abide by.

Within each of these branches are many different schools of thought and still further sub-fields of study.

Meta-ethics

Meta-ethics is the branch of ethics that seeks to understand the nature of ethical properties, and ethical statements, attitudes, and judgments.

Health

At the time of the creation of the World Health Organization (WHO), in 1948, Health was defined as being `a state of complete physical, mental, and social well-being and not merely the absence of disease or infirmity`.
This definition invited nations to expand the conceptual framework of their Health systems beyond issues related to the physical condition of individuals and their diseases, and it motivated us to focus our attention on what we now call social determinants of Health. Consequently, WHO challenged political, academic, community, and professional organizations devoted to improving or preserving Health to make the scope of their work explicit, including their rationale for allocating resources.

Chapter 7. Benner`s Philosophy in Nursing Practice,

Illness	Illness is a state of poor health. Illness is sometimes considered another word for disease. Others maintain that fine distinctions exist.
Caregiver	Carer (UK, NZ, Australian usage) and Caregiver are words normally used to refer to unpaid relatives or friends who support people with disabilities. The words may be prefixed with `family` `spousal`, `child` to distinguish between different care situations. The general term dependent/dependant care is also used for the service provided.
Stress	Stress is a term in psychology and biology, first coined in the biological context in the 1930s, which has in more recent decades become commonly used in popular parlance. It refers to the consequence of the failure of an organism - human or animal - to respond appropriately to emotional or physical threats, whether actual or imagined. Signs of stress may be cognitive, emotional, physical or behavioral.
Health care	Health care , refers to the treatment and management of illness, and the preservation of health through services offered by the medical, dental, complementary and alternative medicine, pharmaceutical, clinical laboratory sciences , nursing, and allied health professions. Health care embraces all the goods and services designed to promote health, including `preventive, curative and palliative interventions, whether directed to individuals or to populations`. Before the term Health care became popular, English-speakers referred to medicine or to the health sector and spoke of the treatment and prevention of illness and disease.
Nursing diagnosis	A Nursing diagnosis is a standardized statement about the health of a client (who can be an individual, a family, or a community) for the purpose of providing nursing care. Nursing diagnoses are developed based on data obtained during the nursing assessment. The main organization for defining standard diagnoses in North America is the North American Nursing diagnosis Association, now known as NANDA-International.
Nursing research	Nursing research is the term used to describe the evidence used to support nursing practice. Nursing, as an evidence based area of practice, has been developing since the time of Florence Nightingale to the present day, where many nurses now work as researchers based in universities as well as in the health care setting.

Chapter 7. Benner`s Philosophy in Nursing Practice,

Nurse education places emphasis upon the use of evidence from research in order to rationalise nursing interventions.

Role

A Role or a social Role is a set of connected behaviors, rights and obligations as conceptualized by actors in a social situation. It is an expected or free or continously changing behavior and may have a given individual social status or social position. It is vital to both functionalist and interactionist understandings of society. Social Role posits the following about social behavior:

· The division of labor in society takes the form of the interaction among heterogeneous specialized positions, we call Roles.

· Social Roles included appropriate and permitted forms of behavior, guided by social norms, which are commonly known and hence determine the expectations for appropriate behavior in these Roles.

· Roles are occupied by individuals, who are called actors.

· When individuals approve of a social Role (i.e., they consider the Role legitimate and constructive, they will incur costs to conform to Role norms, and will also incur costs to punish those who violate Role norms.

· Changed conditions can render a social Role outdated or illegitimate, in which case social pressures are likely to lead to Role change.

· The anticipation of rewards and punishments, as well as the satisfaction of behaving prosocially, account for why agents conform to Role requirmeets.

Customer

A customer buyer, is usually used to refer to a current or potential buyer or user of the products of an individual or organization, called the supplier, seller, or vendor. This is typically through purchasing or renting goods or services. However, in certain contexts, the term customer also includes by extension anyone who uses or experiences the services of another.

Chapter 7. Benner`s Philosophy in Nursing Practice,

Management	Management in all business and organizational activities is the act of getting people together to accomplish desired goals and objectives using available resources efficiently and effectively. Management comprises planning, organizing, staffing, leading or directing, and controlling an organization (a group of one or more people or entities) or effort for the purpose of accomplishing a goal. Resourcing encompasses the deployment and manipulation of human resources, financial resources, technological resources, and natural resources.
Monitoring	To monitor or Monitoring generally means to be aware of the state of a system. Below are specific examples:

· to observe a situation for any changes which may occur over time, using a monitor or measuring device of some sort:

· Baby monitor, medical monitor, Heart rate monitor

· BioMonitoring

· Cure Monitoring for composite materials manufacturing

· Deformation Monitoring

· Election Monitoring

· Mining Monitoring

· Natural hazard Monitoring

· Network Monitoring

· Structural Monitoring

· Website Monitoring

· Futures Monitoring, Media Monitoring service

· to observe the behaviour or communications of individuals or groups

· Monitoring competence at a task.

· Clinical Monitoring for new medical drugs
Monitoring Integration Platform

· Indiktor - Monitoring Integration Platform

·

Nurse	A Nurse is a healthcare professional who, in collaboration with other members of a health care team, is responsible for: treatment, safety, and recovery of acutely or chronically ill individuals; health promotion and maintenance within families, communities and populations; and, treatment of life-threatening emergencies in a wide range of health care settings. Nurses perform a wide range of clinical and non-clinical functions necessary to the delivery of health care, and may also be involved in medical and nursing research.

Both Nursing roles and education were first defined by Florence Nightingale, following her experiences caring for the wounded in the Crimean War. |
| Telerobotics | Telerobotics is the area of robotics concerned with the control of robots from a distance, chiefly using wireless connections (like Wi-Fi, Bluetooth, the Deep Space Network, and similar), `tethered` connections, teleoperation and telepresence.
Teleoperation means `doing work at a distance`, although `work` may mean almost anything. |
| Clinical practice | Good Clinical practice is an international quality standard that is provided by International Conference on Harmonisation (ICH), an international body that defines standards, which governments can transpose into regulations for clinical trials involving human subjects.

Good Clinical practice guidelines include protection of human rights as a subject in clinical trial. It also provides assurance of the safety and efficacy of the newly developed compounds. |

Chapter 7. Benner`s Philosophy in Nursing Practice,

Skill	A Skill is the learned capacity to carry out pre-determined results often with the minimum outlay of time, energy, or both. Skills can often be divided into domain-general and domain-specific Skills. For example, in the domain of work, some general Skills would include time management, teamwork and leadership, self motivation and others, whereas domain-specific Skills would be useful only for a certain job.
Nursing theory	Nursing theory is the term given to the body of knowledge that is used to define or explain various aspects of the profession of nursing. Types of nursing theories Grand nursing theories Grand nursing theories have the broadest scope and present general concepts and propositions. Theories at this level may both reflect and provide insights useful for practice but are not designed for empirical testing.
Knowledge	Knowledge is defined by the Oxford English Dictionary as (i) expertise, and skills acquired by a person through experience or education; the theoretical or practical understanding of a subject; (ii) what is known in a particular field or in total; facts and information; or (iii) be absolutely certain or sure about something. Philosophical debates in general start with Plato's formulation of knowledge as "justified true belief." There is however no single agreed definition of knowledge presently, nor any prospect of one, and there remain numerous competing theories. Knowledge acquisition involves complex cognitive processes: perception, learning, communication, association and reasoning.
Arthritis	Arthritis is a group of conditions involving damage to the joints of the body. There are over 100 different forms of arthritis. The most common form, osteoarthritis is a result of trauma to the joint, infection of the joint, or age.

Chapter 7. Benner's Philosophy in Nursing Practice,

Clinical nurse specialist	A clinical nurse specialist is an advanced practice nurse, with graduate preparation (earned master's or doctorate) from a program that prepares Clinical nurse specialists. Clinical nurse specialists are clinical experts in a specialized area of nursing practice and in the delivery of evidence-based nursing interventions. Overview Clinical nurse specialists work with other nurses to advance their nursing practices, improve outcomes, and provide clinical expertise to effect system-wide changes to improve programs of care.
Ambulatory care	Ambulatory care is any medical care delivered on an outpatient basis. Many medical conditions do not require hospital admission and can be managed without admission to a hospital. Many medical investigations can be performed on an ambulatory basis, including blood tests, X-rays, endoscopy and even biopsy procedures of superficial organs.
Ambulatory care nursing	Ambulatory care nursing is characterized by rapid, focused assessments of patients, long-term nurse/patient/family relationships and teaching and translating prescriptions for care into doable activities for patients and their caregivers. Ambulatory care nurses work in outpatient settings, responding to high volumes of patients in short term spans while dealing with issues that are not always predictable. The specialty spans all populations of patients, and care ranges from wellness/prevention to illness and support of the dying.
Breastfeeding	Breastfeeding is the feeding of an infant or young child with breast milk directly from female human breasts (i.e., via lactation) rather than from a baby bottle or other container. Babies have a sucking reflex that enables them to suck and swallow milk. Most mothers can breastfeed for six months or more, without the addition of infant formula or solid food.

Chapter 7. Benner's Philosophy in Nursing Practice,

Hare Krishna	The Hare Krishna mantra, also referred to reverentially as the Maha Mantra ("Great Mantra"), is a sixteen-word Vaishnava mantra which first appeared in the Kali-Santarana Upanishad, and which from the 15th century rose to importance in the Bhakti movement following the teachings of Chaitanya Mahaprabhu. According to Gaudiya Vaishnava theology, one's original consciousness and goal of life is pure love of God (Krishna). Since the 1960s, the mantra has been made well known outside of India by A. C. Bhaktivedanta Swami Prabhupada and his International Society for Krishna Consciousness (commonly known as "the Hare Krishnas").
Nurse practitioner	A Nurse Practitioner is an Advanced Practice Nurse (APN) who has completed graduate-level education (either a Master's or a Doctoral degree). Additional APN roles include the Certified Registered Nurse Anesthetist (CRNA)s, CNMs, and CNSs. All Nurse Practitioners are Registered Nurses who have completed extensive additional education, training, and have a dramatically expanded scope of practice over the traditional RN role.
Theory	Originally the word theory is a technical term from Ancient Greek. It is derived from theoria, θεωρ? α, meaning "a looking at, viewing, beholding", and refers to contemplation or speculation, as opposed to action. Theory is especially often contrasted to "practice" a concept that in its original Aristotelian context referred to actions done for their own sake, but can also refer to "technical" actions instrumental to some other aim, such as the making of tools or houses.
Disease	A disease is an abnormal condition affecting the body of an organism. It is often construed to be a medical condition associated with specific symptoms and signs. It may be caused by external factors, such as infectious disease, or it may be caused by internal dysfunctions, such as autoimmune diseases.
Reasoning	Reasoning is the cognitive process of looking for reasons, beliefs, conclusions, actions or feelings. Different forms of such reflection on Reasoning occur in different fields. In philosophy, the study of Reasoning typically focuses on what makes Reasoning efficient or inefficient, appropriate or inappropriate, good or bad.

Chapter 7. Benner`s Philosophy in Nursing Practice,

Case management	Case management is the coordination of community services for mental health patients by allocating a professional to be responsible for the assessment of need and implementation of care plans. It is usually most appropriate for people who, as a result of a serious mental illness, have ongoing support needs in areas such as housing, employment, social relationships, and community participation. In particular, service users with a major psychotic disorder are most often suited to receiving services within this model.
Case study	A case study is a research method common in social science. It is based on an in-depth investigation of a single individual, group, or event. Case studies may be descriptive or explanatory.
Cervical	In anatomy, `Cervical` is an adjective that has two meanings: · of or pertaining to any neck. · of or pertaining to the female cervix: i.e., the neck of the uterus. · Commonly used medical phrases involving the neck are · Cervical collar · Cervical disc (intervertebral disc) · Cervical lymph nodes · Cervical nerves · Cervical vertebrae · Cervical rib · Phrases that involve the cervix include

Chapter 7. Benner's Philosophy in Nursing Practice,

· Cervical cancer

· Cervical smear or Pap smear

Cervical cancer	Cervical cancer is malignant neoplasm of the cervix uteri or cervical area. It may present with vaginal bleeding, but symptoms may be absent until the cancer is in its advanced stages. Treatment consists of surgery (including local excision) in early stages and chemotherapy and radiotherapy in advanced stages of the disease.
Gaze	The term gaze is frequently used in physiology to describe coordinated motion of the eyes and neck. The lateral gaze is controlled by the paramedian pontine reticular formation (PPRF). The vertical gaze is controlled by the rostral interstitial nucleus of medial longitudinal fasciculus and the interstitial nucleus of Cajal.
Oncology	Oncology (from the Ancient Greek onkos (?γκος), meaning bulk, mass, or tumor, and the suffix -logy (-λογ?α), meaning "study of") is a branch of medicine that deals with tumors (cancer). A medical professional who practices oncology is an oncologist.

Oncology is concerned with:

- The diagnosis of any cancer in a person
- Therapy (e.g., surgery, chemotherapy, radiotherapy and other modalities)
- Follow-up of cancer patients after successful treatment
- Palliative care of patients with terminal malignancies
- Ethical questions surrounding cancer care
- Screening efforts:
  - of populations, or
  - of the relatives of patients (in types of cancer that are thought to have a hereditary basis, such as breast cancer)

Diagnosis

The most important diagnostic tool remains the medical history: the character of the complaints and any specific symptoms (fatigue, weight loss, unexplained anemia, fever of unknown origin, paraneoplastic phenomena and other signs).

Chapter 7. Benner's Philosophy in Nursing Practice,

Fatty liver	Fatty liver, also known as Fatty liver disease (Fatty liverD), steatorrhoeic hepatosis, steatosis hepatitis and hepatosteatosis, is a reversible condition where large vacuoles of triglyceride fat accumulate in liver cells via the process of steatosis. Despite having multiple causes, Fatty liver can be considered a single disease that occurs worldwide in those with excessive alcohol intake and those who are obese (with or without effects of insulin resistance). The condition is also associated with other diseases that influence fat metabolism.
Situated	In artificial intelligence and cognitive science, the term situated refers to an agent which is embedded in an environment. In this used, the term is used to refer to robots, but some researchers argue that software agents can also be situated if: · they exist in a dynamic (rapidly changing) environment, which · they can manipulate or change through their actions, and which · they can sense or perceive. Being situated is generally considered to be part of being embodied, but it is useful to take both perspectives.
Acute	In medicine, an acute disease is a disease with either or both of: 1. a rapid onset, as in acute infection 2. a short course (as opposed to a chronic course). This adjective is part of the definition of several diseases and is, therefore, incorporated in their name, for instance, severe acute respiratory syndrome, acute leukemia. The term acute may often be confused by the general public to mean 'severe'. This however, is a different characteristic and something can be acute but not severe.
Pregnancy	Pregnancy is the carrying of one or more offspring, known as a fetus or embryo, inside the womb of a female. In a pregnancy, there can be multiple gestations, as in the case of twins or triplets. Human pregnancy is the most studied of all mammalian pregnancies.

Chapter 8. Johnson`s Behavioral System Model in Nursing Practice,

Humans	Humans commonly refers to the species Homo sapiens , the only extant member of the Homo genus of bipedal primates in Hominidae, the great ape family. However, in some cases the term is used to refer to any member of the genus Homo.
	Humans have a highly developed brain, capable of abstract reasoning, language, introspection, and problem solving.
Science of Unitary Human Beings	The science of unitary human beings is a grand nursing theory developed by Martha E. Rogers. The details of the theory are included in her book, An Introduction to the Theoretical Basis of Nursing.
	Overview
	According to Rogers, Nursing is both a science and an art.
Education	Education in the largest sense is any act or experience that has a formative effect on the mind, character or physical ability of an individual. In its technical sense, education is the process by which society deliberately transmits its accumulated knowledge, skills and values from one generation to another.
	Etymologically, the word education is derived from educare "bring up", which is related to educere "bring out", "bring forth what is within", "bring out potential" and ducere, "to lead".
Case study	A case study is a research method common in social science. It is based on an in-depth investigation of a single individual, group, or event. Case studies may be descriptive or explanatory.

Chapter 8. Johnson`s Behavioral System Model in Nursing Practice,

Assessment	Educational Assessment is the process of documenting, usually in measurable terms, knowledge, skills, attitudes and beliefs. Assessment can focus on the individual learner, the learning community (class, workshop, or other organized group of learners), the institution, or the educational system as a whole. According to the Academic Exchange Quarterly: 'Studies of a theoretical or empirical nature addressing the Assessment of learner aptitude and preparation, motivation and learning styles, learning outcomes in achievement and satisfaction in different educational contexts are all welcome, as are studies addressing issues of measurable standards and benchmarks'.
Nursing	Nursing is a healthcare profession focused on the care of individuals, families, and communities so they may attain, maintain, or recover optimal health and quality of life from conception to death.
	Nurses work in a large variety of specialties where they work independently and as part of a team to assess, plan, implement and evaluate care. Nursing Science is a field of knowledge based on the contributions of nursing scientist through peer reviewed scholarly journals and evidenced-based practice.
Healing	Physiological healing is the restoration of damaged living tissue to normal function. It is the process by which the cells in the body regenerate and repair to reduce the size of a damaged or necrotic area. Healing incorporates both the removal of necrotic tissue (demolition), and the replacement of this tissue.
Nursing diagnosis	A Nursing diagnosis is a standardized statement about the health of a client (who can be an individual, a family, or a community) for the purpose of providing nursing care. Nursing diagnoses are developed based on data obtained during the nursing assessment.
	The main organization for defining standard diagnoses in North America is the North American Nursing diagnosis Association, now known as NANDA-International.
Nursing Process	The nursing process is a process by which nurses deliver care to individuals, families, and/or communities and is supported by nursing theories. The nursing process was originally an adapted form of problem-solving and is classified as a deductive theory.
	Phases of the nursing process

Chapter 8. Johnson`s Behavioral System Model in Nursing Practice,

	The nursing process is a client-centered, goal-oriented method of caring that provides a framework to nursing care.
Theory	Originally the word theory is a technical term from Ancient Greek. It is derived from theoria, θεωρ?α, meaning "a looking at, viewing, beholding", and refers to contemplation or speculation, as opposed to action. Theory is especially often contrasted to "practice" a concept that in its original Aristotelian context referred to actions done for their own sake, but can also refer to "technical" actions instrumental to some other aim, such as the making of tools or houses.
Hare Krishna	The Hare Krishna mantra, also referred to reverentially as the Maha Mantra ("Great Mantra"), is a sixteen-word Vaishnava mantra which first appeared in the Kali-Santarana Upanishad, and which from the 15th century rose to importance in the Bhakti movement following the teachings of Chaitanya Mahaprabhu.

According to Gaudiya Vaishnava theology, one's original consciousness and goal of life is pure love of God (Krishna). Since the 1960s, the mantra has been made well known outside of India by A. C. Bhaktivedanta Swami Prabhupada and his International Society for Krishna Consciousness (commonly known as "the Hare Krishnas"). |
| Family | Family is a group of people or animals (many species form the equivalent of a human Family wherein the adults care for the young) affiliated by consanguinity, affinity or co-residence. Although the concept of consanguinity originally referred to relations by `blood`, anthropologists have argued that one must understand the idea of `blood` metaphorically and that many societies understand Family through other concepts rather than through genetic distance.

One of the primary functions of the Family is to produce and reproduce persons, biologically and socially. |

Chapter 8. Johnson's Behavioral System Model in Nursing Practice,

Role	A Role or a social Role is a set of connected behaviors, rights and obligations as conceptualized by actors in a social situation. It is an expected or free or continously changing behavior and may have a given individual social status or social position. It is vital to both functionalist and interactionist understandings of society. Social Role posits the following about social behavior:

· The division of labor in society takes the form of the interaction among heterogeneous specialized positions, we call Roles.

· Social Roles included appropriate and permitted forms of behavior, guided by social norms, which are commonly known and hence determine the expectations for appropriate behavior in these Roles.

· Roles are occupied by individuals, who are called actors.

· When individuals approve of a social Role (i.e., they consider the Role legitimate and constructive, they will incur costs to conform to Role norms, and will also incur costs to punish those who violate Role norms.

· Changed conditions can render a social Role outdated or illegitimate, in which case social pressures are likely to lead to Role change.

· The anticipation of rewards and punishments, as well as the satisfaction of behaving prosocially, account for why agents conform to Role requirmeets.

Social	The term Social refers to a characteristic of living organisms (humans in particular, though biologists also apply the term to populations of other animals). It always refers to the interaction of organisms with other organisms and to their collective co-existence, irrespective of whether they are aware of it or not, and irrespective of whether the interaction is voluntary or involuntary.

In the absence of agreement about its meaning, the term `Social` is used in many different senses and regarded as a fuzzy concept, referring among other things to:

· Attitudes, orientations, or behaviours which take the interests, intentions, or needs of other people into account (in contrast to anti-Social behaviour);has played some role in defining the idea or the principle. For instance terms like Social realism, Social justice, Social constructivism, Social psychology and Social capital imply that there is some Social process involved or considered, a process that is not there in regular, `non-Social`, realism, justice, constructivism, psychology, or capital.

Cognitive dysfunction	Cognitive dysfunction is defined as unusually poor mental function, associated with confusion, forgetfulness and difficulty concentrating. A number of medical or psychiatric conditions and treatments can cause such symptoms, including heavy metal poisoning (in particular mercury poisoning), menopause, fibromyalgia, ADHD and sleep disorders (including disrupted sleep). The term brain fog is not commonly used to describe people with dementia or other conditions that are known to cause confusion and memory problems, but it can be used as a synonym for sleep inertia or grogginess upon being awakened from deep sleep.
Collaboration	Collaboration is a recursive process where two or more people or organizations work together in an intersection of common goals -- for example, an intellectual endeavor that is creative in nature--by sharing knowledge, learning and building consensus. Most Collaboration requires leadership, although the form of leadership can be social within a decentralized and egalitarian group. In particular, teams that work collaboratively can obtain greater resources, recognition and reward when facing competition for finite resources.
Interventions	Interventions is a book by Noam Chomsky, an American linguist, MIT professor, and political activist. Published in May 2007, Interventions is a collection of 44 op-ed articles, post-9/11, from September 2002, through March 2007. After 9/11, Noam Chomsky began writing short, roughly 1000 word concise articles, distributed by The New York Times Syndicate as op-eds. They were widely picked up overseas but rarely in the US and only in smaller regional or local papers.
Hypernatremia	Hypernatremia or hypernatraemia is an electrolyte disturbance that is defined by an elevated sodium level in the blood. Hypernatremia is generally not caused by an excess of sodium, but rather by a relative deficit of free water in the body. For this reason, Hypernatremia is often synonymous with the less precise term, dehydration.

Kidney	As distinct from the Western medical concept of Kidneys, this concept from Traditional Chinese Medicine is more a way of describing a set of interrelated parts than an anatomical organ.
	To differentiate between western or eastern concepts of organs the first letter is capitalized (Liver, instead of liver, Spleen instead of spleen). Because Traditional Chinese Medicine (TCM) is holistic, each organ cannot be explained fully unless the TCM relationship/homeostasis with the other organs is understood.
Cancer	Cancer (medical term: malignant neoplasm) is a class of diseases in which a group of cells display uncontrolled growth, invasion that intrudes upon and destroys adjacent tissues, and sometimes metastasis, or spreading to other locations in the body via lymph or blood. These three malignant properties of cancers differentiate them from benign tumors, which do not invade or metastasize.
	Researchers divide the causes of cancer into two groups: those with an environmental cause and those with a hereditary genetic cause.
Clinical Trial	Clinical trials are conducted to allow safety (or more specifically, information about adverse drug reactions and adverse effects of other treatments) and efficacy data to be collected for health interventions (e.g., drugs, diagnostics, devices, therapy protocols). These trials can take place only after satisfactory information has been gathered on the quality of the non-clinical safety, and Health Authority/Ethics Committee approval is granted in the country where the trial is taking place.
	Depending on the type of product and the stage of its development, investigators enroll healthy volunteers and/or patients into small pilot studies initially, followed by larger scale studies in patients that often compare the new product with the currently prescribed treatment.

Chapter 9. King`s Conceptual System and Theory of Goal Attainment in Nursing,

Empathy	Empathy is the capacity to recognize and, to some extent, share feelings (such as sadness or happiness) that are being experienced by another semi-sentient being. Someone may need to have a certain amount of empathy before they are able to feel compassion. Etymology The English word is derived from the Greek word ?μπ?θεια (empatheia), "physical affection, passion, partiality" which comes from ?v (en), "in, at" + π?θος (pathos), "passion" or "suffering".
Goal	Goal refers to a method of scoring in many sports. It can also refer to the physical structure or area of the playing surface in which a score is made. The structure of a Goal can vary widely from sport to sport.
Learning	Learning is acquiring new or modifying existing knowledge, behaviors, skills, values, or preferences and may involve synthesizing different types of information. The ability to learn is possessed by humans, animals and some machines. Progress over time tends to follow learning curves.
Self-Awareness	Self-awareness is literally consciousness of one`s self. It is related to but not identical with self-consciousness  I think, therefore I am  `...And as I observed that this truth `I think, therefore I am` (Cogito ergo sum) was so certain and of such evidence ...I concluded that I might, without scruple, accept it as the first principle of the Philosophy I was in search.`  `...In the statement `I think, therefore I am` ...I see very clearly that to think it is necessary to be, I concluded that I might take, as a general rule, the principle, that all the things which we very clearly and distinctly conceive are true...`

Chapter 9. King's Conceptual System and Theory of Goal Attainment in Nursing,

	While reading Descartes, Locke began to relish the great ideas of philosophy and the scientific method. On one occasion, while in a meeting with friends, the question of the `limits of human understanding` arose.
Social	The term Social refers to a characteristic of living organisms (humans in particular, though biologists also apply the term to populations of other animals). It always refers to the interaction of organisms with other organisms and to their collective co-existence, irrespective of whether they are aware of it or not, and irrespective of whether the interaction is voluntary or involuntary. In the absence of agreement about its meaning, the term `Social` is used in many different senses and regarded as a fuzzy concept, referring among other things to: · Attitudes, orientations, or behaviours which take the interests, intentions, or needs of other people into account (in contrast to anti-Social behaviour);has played some role in defining the idea or the principle. For instance terms like Social realism, Social justice, Social constructivism, Social psychology and Social capital imply that there is some Social process involved or considered, a process that is not there in regular, `non-Social`, realism, justice, constructivism, psychology, or capital.
Theory	Originally the word theory is a technical term from Ancient Greek. It is derived from theoria, θεωρ? α, meaning "a looking at, viewing, beholding", and refers to contemplation or speculation, as opposed to action. Theory is especially often contrasted to "practice" a concept that in its original Aristotelian context referred to actions done for their own sake, but can also refer to "technical" actions instrumental to some other aim, such as the making of tools or houses.
Womanhood	Womanhood is the period in a female`s life after she has transitioned from girlhood, at least physically, having passed the age of menarche. Many cultures have rites of passage to symbolize a woman`s coming of age, such as confirmation in some branches of Christianity, bat mitzvah in Judaism, or even just the custom of a special celebration for a certain birthday (generally between 12 and 21). The word woman can be used generally, to mean any female human, or specifically, to mean an adult female human as contrasted with girl.

Chapter 9. King`s Conceptual System and Theory of Goal Attainment in Nursing,

Nursing	Nursing is a healthcare profession focused on the care of individuals, families, and communities so they may attain, maintain, or recover optimal health and quality of life from conception to death.
	Nurses work in a large variety of specialties where they work independently and as part of a team to assess, plan, implement and evaluate care. Nursing Science is a field of knowledge based on the contributions of nursing scientist through peer reviewed scholarly journals and evidenced-based practice.
Selection	In the context of evolution, certain traits or alleles of genes segregating within a population may be subject to selection. Under selection, individuals with advantageous or "adaptive" traits tend to be more successful than their peers reproductively--meaning they contribute more offspring to the succeeding generation than others do. When these traits have a genetic basis, selection can increase the prevalence of those traits, because offspring will inherit those traits from their parents.
Communication	Communication is a process of transferring information from one entity to another. Communication processes are sign-mediated interactions between at least two agents which share a repertoire of signs and semiotic rules. Communication is commonly defined as `the imparting or interchange of thoughts, opinions, or information by speech, writing, or signs`.
Humans	Humans commonly refers to the species Homo sapiens , the only extant member of the Homo genus of bipedal primates in Hominidae, the great ape family. However, in some cases the term is used to refer to any member of the genus Homo.
	Humans have a highly developed brain, capable of abstract reasoning, language, introspection, and problem solving.
Interaction	Interaction is a kind of action that occurs as two or more objects have an effect upon one another. The idea of a two-way effect is essential in the concept of interaction, as opposed to a one-way causal effect. A closely related term is interconnectivity, which deals with the interactions of interactions within systems: combinations of many simple interactions can lead to surprising emergent phenomena.

Chapter 9. King`s Conceptual System and Theory of Goal Attainment in Nursing,

Personal space	Personal space is the region surrounding a person which they regard as psychologically theirs. Invasion of Personal space often leads to discomfort, anger, or anxiety on the part of the victim. The notion of Personal space comes from Edward T. Hall, whose ideas were influenced by Heini Hediger`s studies of behavior of zoo animals.
Role	A Role or a social Role is a set of connected behaviors, rights and obligations as conceptualized by actors in a social situation. It is an expected or free or continously changing behavior and may have a given individual social status or social position. It is vital to both functionalist and interactionist understandings of society. Social Role posits the following about social behavior: · The division of labor in society takes the form of the interaction among heterogeneous specialized positions, we call Roles. · Social Roles included appropriate and permitted forms of behavior, guided by social norms, which are commonly known and hence determine the expectations for appropriate behavior in these Roles. · Roles are occupied by individuals, who are called actors. · When individuals approve of a social Role (i.e., they consider the Role legitimate and constructive, they will incur costs to conform to Role norms, and will also incur costs to punish those who violate Role norms. · Changed conditions can render a social Role outdated or illegitimate, in which case social pressures are likely to lead to Role change. · The anticipation of rewards and punishments, as well as the satisfaction of behaving prosocially, account for why agents conform to Role requirmeets.
Caregiver	Carer (UK, NZ, Australian usage) and Caregiver are words normally used to refer to unpaid relatives or friends who support people with disabilities. The words may be prefixed with `family` `spousal`, `child` to distinguish between different care situations. The general term dependent/dependant care is also used for the service provided.
Healing	Physiological healing is the restoration of damaged living tissue to normal function. It is the process by which the cells in the body regenerate and repair to reduce the size of a damaged or necrotic area. Healing incorporates both the removal of necrotic tissue (demolition), and the replacement of this tissue.

Clam\ol

Chapter 9. King`s Conceptual System and Theory of Goal Attainment in Nursing,

Image	An image is an artifact, for example a two-dimensional picture, that has a similar appearance to some subject--usually a physical object or a person. Characteristics Images may be two-dimensional, such as a photograph, screen display, and as well as a three-dimensional, such as a statue or hologram. They may be captured by optical devices--such as cameras, mirrors, lenses, telescopes, microscopes, etc.
Assessment	Educational Assessment is the process of documenting, usually in measurable terms, knowledge, skills, attitudes and beliefs. Assessment can focus on the individual learner, the learning community (class, workshop, or other organized group of learners), the institution, or the educational system as a whole. According to the Academic Exchange Quarterly: 'Studies of a theoretical or empirical nature addressing the Assessment of learner aptitude and preparation, motivation and learning styles, learning outcomes in achievement and satisfaction in different educational contexts are all welcome, as are studies addressing issues of measurable standards and benchmarks'.
Case study	A case study is a research method common in social science. It is based on an in-depth investigation of a single individual, group, or event. Case studies may be descriptive or explanatory.
Extracorporeal	An extracorporeal medical procedure is a medical procedure which is performed outside the body. Circulatory procedures A procedure in which blood is taken from a patient's circulation to have a process applied to it before it is returned to the circulation. All of the apparatus carrying the blood outside the body is termed the extracorporeal circuit.

Chapter 9. King`s Conceptual System and Theory of Goal Attainment in Nursing,

Extracorporeal membrane oxygenation	In intensive care medicine, extracorporeal membrane oxygenation is an extracorporeal technique of providing both cardiac and respiratory support oxygen to patients whose heart and lungs are so severely diseased or damaged that they can no longer serve their function. Uses One of the new uses is in adults and children with the H1N1 flu. It is also used with children who have respiratory syncytial virus infections.
Neonatal intensive care unit	A neonatal intensive care unit, usually shortened neonatal intensive care unit and also called a newborn intensive care unit, intensive care nursery , and special care baby unit , is a unit of a hospital specializing in the care of ill or premature newborn infants. The neonatal intensive care unit is distinct from a special care nursery (SCN) in providing a high level of intensive care to premature infants while the SCN provides specialized care for infants with less severe medical problems. neonatal intensive care units were developed in the 1950s and 1960s by pediatricians to provide better temperature support, isolation from infection risk, specialized feeding, and greater access to specialized equipment and resources.
Intensive care	Intensive care medicine or critical care medicine is a branch of medicine concerned with the provision of life support or organ support systems in patients who are critically ill and who usually require intensive monitoring. Patients requiring intensive care may require support for hemodynamic instability (hypertension/hypotension), airway or respiratory compromise (such as ventilator support), acute renal failure, potentially lethal cardiac arrhythmias, or the cumulative effects of multiple organ system failure. They may also be admitted for intensive/invasive monitoring, such as the crucial hours after major surgery when deemed too unstable to transfer to a less intensively monitored unit.
Membrane	A Membrane is a layer of material which serves as a selective barrier between two phases and remains impermeable to specific particles, molecules, or substances when exposed to the action of a driving force. Some components are allowed passage by the Membrane into a permeate stream, whereas others are retained by it and accumulate in the retentate stream.

Membranes can be of various thickness, with homogeneous or heterogeneous structure.

Perception	In philosophy, psychology, and cognitive science, perception is the process of attaining awareness or understanding of sensory information. The word "perception" comes from the Latin words perceptio, percipio, and means "receiving, collecting, action of taking possession, apprehension with the mind or senses." Perception is one of the oldest fields in psychology. The oldest quantitative law in psychology is the Weber-Fechner law, which quantifies the relationship between the intensity of physical stimuli and their perceptual effects.

Chapter 10. Levine's Conservation Model in Nursing Practice,

Nursing	Nursing is a healthcare profession focused on the care of individuals, families, and communities so they may attain, maintain, or recover optimal health and quality of life from conception to death.
	Nurses work in a large variety of specialties where they work independently and as part of a team to assess, plan, implement and evaluate care. Nursing Science is a field of knowledge based on the contributions of nursing scientist through peer reviewed scholarly journals and evidenced-based practice.
Burn	A burn is a type of injury to flesh caused by heat, electricity, chemicals, light, radiation or friction. Most burns only affect the skin (epidermal tissue and dermis). Rarely, deeper tissues, such as muscle, bone, and blood vessels can also be injured.
Cancer	Cancer (medical term: malignant neoplasm) is a class of diseases in which a group of cells display uncontrolled growth, invasion that intrudes upon and destroys adjacent tissues, and sometimes metastasis, or spreading to other locations in the body via lymph or blood. These three malignant properties of cancers differentiate them from benign tumors, which do not invade or metastasize.
	Researchers divide the causes of cancer into two groups: those with an environmental cause and those with a hereditary genetic cause.
Exercise	Exercise is activity performed in order to develop or maintain physical fitness and overall health. It is also necessary for improving athletic ability. Frequent and regular physical Exercise helps prevent some diseases of affluence such as heart disease, cardiovascular disease, Type 2 diabetes and obesity. Nowadays these diseases are very common all over the world and everybody should be conscious about this.
Fatigue	Fatigue is a state of awareness describing a range of afflictions, usually associated with physical and/or mental weakness, though varying from a general state of lethargy to a specific work-induced burning sensation within one's muscles. Physical fatigue is the inability to continue functioning at the level of one's normal abilities. It is widespread in everyday life, but usually becomes particularly noticeable during heavy exercise.

Chapter 10. Levine's Conservation Model in Nursing Practice,

Humans	Humans commonly refers to the species Homo sapiens , the only extant member of the Homo genus of bipedal primates in Hominidae, the great ape family. However, in some cases the term is used to refer to any member of the genus Homo. Humans have a highly developed brain, capable of abstract reasoning, language, introspection, and problem solving.
Individual	As commonly used, an Individual is a person or any specific object in a collection. In the 15th century and earlier, and also today within the fields of statistics and metaphysics, Individual means `indivisible`, typically describing any numerically singular thing, but sometimes meaning `a person.` (q.v. `The problem of proper names`). From the seventeenth century on, Individual indicates separateness, as in Individualism.
Pressure	Example reading: $1\ Pa = 1\ N/m^2 = 10^{-5}\ bar = 10.197{\times}10^{-6}\ at = 9.8692{\times}10^{-6}\ atm$, etc. As an example of varying Pressures, a finger can be pressed against a wall without making any lasting impression; however, the same finger pushing a thumbtack can easily damage the wall. Although the force applied to the surface is the same, the thumbtack applies more Pressure because the point concentrates that force into a smaller area.
Science of Unitary Human Beings	The science of unitary human beings is a grand nursing theory developed by Martha E. Rogers. The details of the theory are included in her book, An Introduction to the Theoretical Basis of Nursing. Overview According to Rogers, Nursing is both a science and an art.
Cancer patient	Although every disease has its patients, to be a Cancer patient has a very specific meaning, both to the patients and their relatives and the general public. Often, there is a large amount of misunderstanding surrounding cancer diagnosis, treatment and follow-up. A diagnosis of cancer is by no means a death warrant.

Chapter 10. Levine`s Conservation Model in Nursing Practice,

Cervical	In anatomy, `Cervical` is an adjective that has two meanings:
	· of or pertaining to any neck.
	· of or pertaining to the female cervix: i.e., the neck of the uterus.
	· Commonly used medical phrases involving the neck are
	· Cervical collar
	· Cervical disc (intervertebral disc)
	· Cervical lymph nodes
	· Cervical nerves
	· Cervical vertebrae
	· Cervical rib
	· Phrases that involve the cervix include
	· Cervical cancer
	· Cervical smear or Pap smear

Chapter 10. Levine`s Conservation Model in Nursing Practice,

Knowledge	Knowledge is defined by the Oxford English Dictionary as (i) expertise, and skills acquired by a person through experience or education; the theoretical or practical understanding of a subject; (ii) what is known in a particular field or in total; facts and information; or (iii) be absolutely certain or sure about something. Philosophical debates in general start with Plato's formulation of knowledge as "justified true belief." There is however no single agreed definition of knowledge presently, nor any prospect of one, and there remain numerous competing theories. Knowledge acquisition involves complex cognitive processes: perception, learning, communication, association and reasoning.
Swaddling	Swaddling is an age-old practice of wrapping infants snugly in swaddling cloths, blankets or similar cloth so that movement of the limbs is tightly restricted. swaddling bands were often used to further restrict the infant. It was commonly believed that this was essential for the infants to develop proper posture.
Acute	In medicine, an acute disease is a disease with either or both of: 1. a rapid onset, as in acute infection 2. a short course (as opposed to a chronic course). This adjective is part of the definition of several diseases and is, therefore, incorporated in their name, for instance, severe acute respiratory syndrome, acute leukemia. The term acute may often be confused by the general public to mean 'severe'. This however, is a different characteristic and something can be acute but not severe.
Energy	Mental or psychic energy is the concept of a principle of activity powering the operation of the mind or psyche. Many modern psychologists or neuroscientists would equate it with increased metabolism in neurons of the brain. Philosophical accounts The idea harks back to Aristotle's conception of actus et potentia.

Chapter 10. Levine`s Conservation Model in Nursing Practice,

Kawasaki disease	Kawasaki disease also known as Kawasaki syndrome, lymph node syndrome and Mucocutaneous lymph node syndrome, is an autoimmune disease that manifests as a systemic necrotizing medium-sized vessel vasculitis and is largely seen in children under 5 years of age. It affects many organ systems, mainly those including the blood vessels, skin, mucous membranes and lymph nodes; however, its most serious effect is on the heart where it can cause severe coronary artery aneurysms in untreated children. Without treatment, mortality may approach 1%, usually within 6 weeks of onset.
Theory	Originally the word theory is a technical term from Ancient Greek. It is derived from theoria, θεωρ? α, meaning "a looking at, viewing, beholding", and refers to contemplation or speculation, as opposed to action. Theory is especially often contrasted to "practice" a concept that in its original Aristotelian context referred to actions done for their own sake, but can also refer to "technical" actions instrumental to some other aim, such as the making of tools or houses.
Ventilation	Ventilation is the intentional movement of air from outside a building to the inside. It is the V in HVAC. With clothes dryers, and combustion equipment such as water heaters, boilers, fireplaces, and wood stoves, their exhausts are often called vents or flues -- this should not be confused with Ventilation. The vents or flues carry the products of combustion which have to be expelled from the building in a way which does not cause harm to the occupants of the building.
Healing	Physiological healing is the restoration of damaged living tissue to normal function. It is the process by which the cells in the body regenerate and repair to reduce the size of a damaged or necrotic area. Healing incorporates both the removal of necrotic tissue (demolition), and the replacement of this tissue.
Health	At the time of the creation of the World Health Organization (WHO), in 1948, Health was defined as being `a state of complete physical, mental, and social well-being and not merely the absence of disease or infirmity`. This definition invited nations to expand the conceptual framework of their Health systems beyond issues related to the physical condition of individuals and their diseases, and it motivated us to focus our attention on what we now call social determinants of Health. Consequently, WHO challenged political, academic, community, and professional organizations devoted to improving or preserving Health to make the scope of their work explicit, including their rationale for allocating resources.
Nursing diagnosis	A Nursing diagnosis is a standardized statement about the health of a client (who can be an individual, a family, or a community) for the purpose of providing nursing care. Nursing diagnoses are developed based on data obtained during the nursing assessment.

Cram
101

Chapter 10. Levine`s Conservation Model in Nursing Practice,

	The main organization for defining standard diagnoses in North America is the North American Nursing diagnosis Association, now known as NANDA-International.
Case study	A case study is a research method common in social science. It is based on an in-depth investigation of a single individual, group, or event. Case studies may be descriptive or explanatory.
House	A House is generally a shelter, building or structure that is a dwelling or place for habitation by human beings. The term includes many kinds of dwellings ranging from rudimentary huts of nomadic tribes to high-rise apartment buildings. In some contexts, `House` may mean the same as dwelling, residence, home, abode, lodging, accommodation, or housing, among other meanings.
Interaction	Interaction is a kind of action that occurs as two or more objects have an effect upon one another. The idea of a two-way effect is essential in the concept of interaction, as opposed to a one-way causal effect. A closely related term is interconnectivity, which deals with the interactions of interactions within systems: combinations of many simple interactions can lead to surprising emergent phenomena.
Nursing theory	Nursing theory is the term given to the body of knowledge that is used to define or explain various aspects of the profession of nursing. Types of nursing theories Grand nursing theories Grand nursing theories have the broadest scope and present general concepts and propositions. Theories at this level may both reflect and provide insights useful for practice but are not designed for empirical testing.
Intention	An agent's intention in performing an action is his or her specific purpose in doing so, the end or goal that is aimed at, or intended to accomplish. Whether an action is successful or unsuccessful depends at least on whether the intended result was brought about. Other consequences of someone's acting are called unintentional.

Chapter 10. Levine`s Conservation Model in Nursing Practice,

Therapeutic	Therapy is the attempted remediation of a health problem, usually following a diagnosis. In the medical field, it is synonymous with the word `treatment`. A therapeutic effect is a consequence of a particular treatment which is judged to be desirable and beneficial.
Empathy	Empathy is the capacity to recognize and, to some extent, share feelings (such as sadness or happiness) that are being experienced by another semi-sentient being. Someone may need to have a certain amount of empathy before they are able to feel compassion. Etymology The English word is derived from the Greek word ?μπ?θεια (empatheia), "physical affection, passion, partiality" which comes from ?v (en), "in, at" + π?θος (pathos), "passion" or "suffering".
Emphysema	Emphysema is a long-term, progressive disease of the lungs that primarily causes shortness of breath. In people with emphysema, the tissues necessary to support the physical shape and function of the lungs are destroyed. It is included in a group of diseases called chronic obstructive pulmonary disease or COPD (pulmonary refers to the lungs).
Health Promotion	Health promotion has been defined by the World Health Organization`s 2005 Bangkok Charter for Health promotion in a Globalized World as `the process of enabling people to increase control over their health and its determinants, and thereby improve their health`. The primary means of Health promotion occur through developing healthy public policy that addresses the prerequisities of health such as income, housing, food security, employment, and quality working conditions. There is a tendency among public health officials and governments -- and this is especially the case in liberal nations such as Canada and the USA -- to reduce Health promotion to health education and social marketing focused on changing behavioral risk factors.
Health care	Health care , refers to the treatment and management of illness, and the preservation of health through services offered by the medical, dental, complementary and alternative medicine, pharmaceutical, clinical laboratory sciences , nursing, and allied health professions. Health care embraces all the goods and services designed to promote health, including `preventive, curative and palliative interventions, whether directed to individuals or to populations`.

Chapter 10. Levine`s Conservation Model in Nursing Practice,

	Before the term Health care became popular, English-speakers referred to medicine or to the health sector and spoke of the treatment and prevention of illness and disease.
Preterm	In humans, preterm birth refers to the birth of a baby of less than 37 weeks gestational age. Premature birth, commonly used as a synonym f birth, refers to the birth of a premature infant. The child may commonly be referred to throughout their life as being born a `preemie` or `preemie baby`.
Skill	A Skill is the learned capacity to carry out pre-determined results often with the minimum outlay of time, energy, or both. Skills can often be divided into domain-general and domain-specific Skills. For example, in the domain of work, some general Skills would include time management, teamwork and leadership, self motivation and others, whereas domain-specific Skills would be useful only for a certain job.
In practice	In Practice is published in conjunction with The Veterinary Record and provides continuing educational material for veterinary practitioners. It focuses on the topics of clinical and practice management. Reviews cover all species, but principally farm and companion animals, providing a regular update on clinical developments.
Monitoring	To monitor or Monitoring generally means to be aware of the state of a system. Below are specific examples: · to observe a situation for any changes which may occur over time, using a monitor or measuring device of some sort: · Baby monitor, medical monitor, Heart rate monitor · BioMonitoring · Cure Monitoring for composite materials manufacturing · Deformation Monitoring · Election Monitoring · Mining Monitoring

· Natural hazard Monitoring

· Network Monitoring

· Structural Monitoring

· Website Monitoring

· Futures Monitoring, Media Monitoring service

· to observe the behaviour or communications of individuals or groups

· Monitoring competence at a task.

· Clinical Monitoring for new medical drugs
Monitoring Integration Platform

· Indiktor - Monitoring Integration Platform

·

Telerobotics	Telerobotics is the area of robotics concerned with the control of robots from a distance, chiefly using wireless connections (like Wi-Fi, Bluetooth, the Deep Space Network, and similar), `tethered` connections, teleoperation and telepresence. Teleoperation means `doing work at a distance`, although `work` may mean almost anything.
Assessment	Educational Assessment is the process of documenting, usually in measurable terms, knowledge, skills, attitudes and beliefs. Assessment can focus on the individual learner, the learning community (class, workshop, or other organized group of learners), the institution, or the educational system as a whole. According to the Academic Exchange Quarterly: 'Studies of a theoretical or empirical nature addressing the Assessment of learner aptitude and preparation, motivation and learning styles, learning outcomes in achievement and satisfaction in different educational contexts are all welcome, as are studies addressing issues of measurable standards and benchmarks'.

Chapter 10. Levine's Conservation Model in Nursing Practice,

Oncology	Oncology (from the Ancient Greek onkos (?γκος), meaning bulk, mass, or tumor, and the suffix -logy (-λογ?α), meaning "study of") is a branch of medicine that deals with tumors (cancer). A medical professional who practices oncology is an oncologist.
	
	Oncology is concerned with:
	
	• The diagnosis of any cancer in a person
	• Therapy (e.g., surgery, chemotherapy, radiotherapy and other modalities)
	• Follow-up of cancer patients after successful treatment
	• Palliative care of patients with terminal malignancies
	• Ethical questions surrounding cancer care
	• Screening efforts:
	    ○ of populations, or
	    ○ of the relatives of patients (in types of cancer that are thought to have a hereditary basis, such as breast cancer)
	
	Diagnosis
	
	The most important diagnostic tool remains the medical history: the character of the complaints and any specific symptoms (fatigue, weight loss, unexplained anemia, fever of unknown origin, paraneoplastic phenomena and other signs).

Cleanliness	Cleanliness is the absence of dirt, including dust, stains, bad smells and garbage. Purposes of Cleanliness include health, beauty, absence of offensive odor, avoidance of shame, and to avoid the spreading of dirt and contaminants to oneself and others. In the case of glass objects such as windows or windshields, the purpose can also be transparency.
Hypotheses	A hypothesis is a proposed explanation for an observable phenomenon. The term derives from the Greek, á½'ποτιθÎναι - hypotithenai meaning `to put under` or `to suppose.` For a hypothesis to be put forward as a scientific hypothesis, the scientific method requires that one can test it. Scientists generally base scientific hypotheses on previous observations that cannot be satisfactorily explained with the available scientific theories.

Chapter 10. Levine`s Conservation Model in Nursing Practice,

Self-Care Deficit Nursing Theory	The self-care deficit nursing theory is a grand nursing theory that was developed between 1959 and 2001 by Dorothea Orem. It is also known as the Orem model of nursing. It is particularly used in rehabilitation and primary care settings where the patient is encouraged to be as independent as possible.
Utilization	Utilization is a statistical concept (Queueing Theory) as well as a primary business measure for the rental industry.
	In queueing theory, utilization is the proportion of the system`s resources which is used by the traffic which arrives at it. It should be strictly less than one for the system to function well.

Chapter 11. Neuman's Systems Model in Nursing Practice,

Nursing	Nursing is a healthcare profession focused on the care of individuals, families, and communities so they may attain, maintain, or recover optimal health and quality of life from conception to death.
	Nurses work in a large variety of specialties where they work independently and as part of a team to assess, plan, implement and evaluate care. Nursing Science is a field of knowledge based on the contributions of nursing scientist through peer reviewed scholarly journals and evidenced-based practice.
Family	Family is a group of people or animals (many species form the equivalent of a human Family wherein the adults care for the young) affiliated by consanguinity, affinity or co-residence. Although the concept of consanguinity originally referred to relations by `blood`, anthropologists have argued that one must understand the idea of `blood` metaphorically and that many societies understand Family through other concepts rather than through genetic distance.
	One of the primary functions of the Family is to produce and reproduce persons, biologically and socially.
Humans	Humans commonly refers to the species Homo sapiens , the only extant member of the Homo genus of bipedal primates in Hominidae, the great ape family. However, in some cases the term is used to refer to any member of the genus Homo.
	Humans have a highly developed brain, capable of abstract reasoning, language, introspection, and problem solving.
Assessment	Educational Assessment is the process of documenting, usually in measurable terms, knowledge, skills, attitudes and beliefs. Assessment can focus on the individual learner, the learning community (class, workshop, or other organized group of learners), the institution, or the educational system as a whole. According to the Academic Exchange Quarterly: 'Studies of a theoretical or empirical nature addressing the Assessment of learner aptitude and preparation, motivation and learning styles, learning outcomes in achievement and satisfaction in different educational contexts are all welcome, as are studies addressing issues of measurable standards and benchmarks'.

Chapter 11. Neuman's Systems Model in Nursing Practice,

Customer	A customer buyer, is usually used to refer to a current or potential buyer or user of the products of an individual or organization, called the supplier, seller, or vendor. This is typically through purchasing or renting goods or services. However, in certain contexts, the term customer also includes by extension anyone who uses or experiences the services of another.
Energy	Mental or psychic energy is the concept of a principle of activity powering the operation of the mind or psyche. Many modern psychologists or neuroscientists would equate it with increased metabolism in neurons of the brain. Philosophical accounts The idea harks back to Aristotle's conception of actus et potentia.
Perspective	Perspective, in context of vision and visual perception, is the way in which objects appear to the eye based on their spatial attributes; or their dimensions and the position of the eye relative to the objects. There are two main meanings of the term: linear perspective and aerial perspective. Linear perspective As objects become more distant they appear smaller because their visual angle decreases.
Theory	Originally the word theory is a technical term from Ancient Greek. It is derived from theoria, θεωρ?α, meaning "a looking at, viewing, beholding", and refers to contemplation or speculation, as opposed to action. Theory is especially often contrasted to "practice" a concept that in its original Aristotelian context referred to actions done for their own sake, but can also refer to "technical" actions instrumental to some other aim, such as the making of tools or houses.
Transformation	In molecular biology, transformation is the genetic alteration of a cell resulting from the uptake, genomic incorporation, and expression of environmental genetic material (DNA). Transformation ransformation occurs most commonly in bacteria, both naturally and artificially, and refers to DNA taken up from the environment through their cell wall. Bacteria that are capable of being transformed are called competent.

Chapter 11. Neuman`s Systems Model in Nursing Practice,

Individual	As commonly used, an Individual is a person or any specific object in a collection. In the 15th century and earlier, and also today within the fields of statistics and metaphysics, Individual means `indivisible`, typically describing any numerically singular thing, but sometimes meaning `a person.` (q.v. `The problem of proper names`). From the seventeenth century on, Individual indicates separateness, as in Individualism.
Resistance	"Resistance" as initially used by Sigmund Freud, referred to patients blocking memories from conscious memory. This was a key concept, since the primary treatment method of Freud's talk therapy required making these memories available to the patient's consciousness. "Resistance" expanded Later, Freud described five different forms of resistance.
Cancer	Cancer (medical term: malignant neoplasm) is a class of diseases in which a group of cells display uncontrolled growth, invasion that intrudes upon and destroys adjacent tissues, and sometimes metastasis, or spreading to other locations in the body via lymph or blood. These three malignant properties of cancers differentiate them from benign tumors, which do not invade or metastasize. Researchers divide the causes of cancer into two groups: those with an environmental cause and those with a hereditary genetic cause.
Clinical Trial	Clinical trials are conducted to allow safety (or more specifically, information about adverse drug reactions and adverse effects of other treatments) and efficacy data to be collected for health interventions (e.g., drugs, diagnostics, devices, therapy protocols). These trials can take place only after satisfactory information has been gathered on the quality of the non-clinical safety, and Health Authority/Ethics Committee approval is granted in the country where the trial is taking place.

Chapter 11. Neuman`s Systems Model in Nursing Practice,

Depending on the type of product and the stage of its development, investigators enroll healthy volunteers and/or patients into small pilot studies initially, followed by larger scale studies in patients that often compare the new product with the currently prescribed treatment.

Normal

· normal, Alabama

· normal, Illinois

· normal a film starring Jessica Lange and Tom Wilkinson

· normal a film by Carl Bessai

· normal or Angels Gone, a Czech film

· normal, a character on Dark Angel

· The normal, a band featuring Daniel Miller

· `normal`, a song by Foo Fighters

· `normal`, a song by Porcupine Tree

· `normal`, a song by The Exies

· normality (concentration), the discrepancy between the concentrations of ionic species in a solution

· Surface normal, a vector (or line) that is perpendicular to a surface

Chapter 11. Neuman`s Systems Model in Nursing Practice,

· normal component, the component of a vector that is perpendicular to a surface

· normal curvature, of a curve on a surface, the component of curvature that is normal to the surface

· normal distribution, a type of probability distribution in probability theory and statistics

· normal extension, in abstract algebra, a certain type of algebraic field extensions

· normal equations, for linear least squares, a model fitting technique using projection matrices

· normal family, a pre-compact family of holomorphic functions

· normal function, a continuous strictly increasing function from ordinals to ordinals

· normal matrix, a matrix which commutes with its conjugate transpose

· normal measure, a particular type of measure on a measurable cardinal

· normal mode, a special type of solution in an oscillating system

· normal morphism, is a morphism that arises as the kernel or cokernel of some other morphisms

· normal number (computing), a number that is within the normal range of a floating-point format

· normal number, a number whose digit sequence is random

· normal operator, a linear operator on a Hilbert space that commutes with its adjoint

· normal polytope, a lattice polytope in which dilation of points is given by summing lattice points

· normal ring, a ring that is its own integral closure in its field of fractions

· normal space, a topological space in which disjoint closed sets can be separated by disjoint neighborhoods

· normal subgroup, a subgroup that is invariant under conjugation in abstract algebra

· normal point, a point on a variety whose local ring is integrally closed

· normal forms, in database normalization, criteria for determining a table`s degree of vulnerability to logical inconsistencies .

Womanhood	Womanhood is the period in a female`s life after she has transitioned from girlhood, at least physically, having passed the age of menarche. Many cultures have rites of passage to symbolize a woman`s coming of age, such as confirmation in some branches of Christianity, bat mitzvah in Judaism, or even just the custom of a special celebration for a certain birthday (generally between 12 and 21). The word woman can be used generally, to mean any female human, or specifically, to mean an adult female human as contrasted with girl.
Caregiver	Carer (UK, NZ, Australian usage) and Caregiver are words normally used to refer to unpaid relatives or friends who support people with disabilities. The words may be prefixed with `family` `spousal`, `child` to distinguish between different care situations. The general term dependent/dependant care is also used for the service provided.
Healing	Physiological healing is the restoration of damaged living tissue to normal function. It is the process by which the cells in the body regenerate and repair to reduce the size of a damaged or necrotic area. Healing incorporates both the removal of necrotic tissue (demolition), and the replacement of this tissue.
Stressor	Stressor is a chemical or biological agent, environmental condition, an external stimulus or an event that causes stress to an organism. An event that triggers the stress response may include for example: • environmental stressors (elevated sound levels, over-illumination, overcrowding) • daily stress events (e.g. traffic, lost keys) • life changes (e.g. divorce, bereavement) • workplace stressors (e.g. role strain, lack of control)
Pressure	Example reading: $1\ Pa = 1\ N/m^2 = 10^{-5}\ bar = 10.197 \times 10^{-6}\ at = 9.8692 \times 10^{-6}\ atm$, etc.

Chapter 11. Neuman`s Systems Model in Nursing Practice,

As an example of varying Pressures, a finger can be pressed against a wall without making any lasting impression; however, the same finger pushing a thumbtack can easily damage the wall. Although the force applied to the surface is the same, the thumbtack applies more Pressure because the point concentrates that force into a smaller area.

Prevention	Prevention refers to: · Preventive medicine · Hazard Prevention, the process of risk study and elimination and mitigation in emergency management · Risk Prevention · Risk management · Preventive maintenance · Crime Prevention · Prevention, an album by Scottish band De Rosa · Prevention a magazine about health in the United States · Prevent (company), a textile company from Slovenia
Nursing diagnosis	A Nursing diagnosis is a standardized statement about the health of a client (who can be an individual, a family, or a community) for the purpose of providing nursing care. Nursing diagnoses are developed based on data obtained during the nursing assessment. The main organization for defining standard diagnoses in North America is the North American Nursing diagnosis Association, now known as NANDA-International.

Chapter 11. Neuman`s Systems Model in Nursing Practice,

Case study	A case study is a research method common in social science. It is based on an in-depth investigation of a single individual, group, or event. Case studies may be descriptive or explanatory.
Omaha System	The Omaha System is a standardized health care terminology consisting of an assessment component (Problem Classification Scheme), an intervention component (Intervention Scheme), and an outcomes component (Problem Rating Scale for Outcomes). Approximately 11,000 interdisciplinary practitioners, educators, and researchers use Omaha System for structured clinical documentation and analysis of secondary data. Omaha System users from Japan, Estonia, Hong Kong, New Zealand, Wales, Canada, The Netherlands, and the United States have presented at international Omaha System conferences.
Taxonomy	Taxonomy is the practice and science of classification. The word finds its roots in the Greek τῐ¬ξῐς, taxis and νῐΟΕμος, nomos (`law` or `science`). Taxonomy uses taxonomic units, known as taxa (singular taxon).
Nursing process	The nursing process is a process by which nurses deliver care to individuals, families, and/or communities and is supported by nursing theories. The nursing process was originally an adapted form of problem-solving and is classified as a deductive theory. Phases of the nursing process The nursing process is a client-centered, goal-oriented method of caring that provides a framework to nursing care.
Health	At the time of the creation of the World Health Organization (WHO), in 1948, Health was defined as being `a state of complete physical, mental, and social well-being and not merely the absence of disease or infirmity`. This definition invited nations to expand the conceptual framework of their Health systems beyond issues related to the physical condition of individuals and their diseases, and it motivated us to focus our attention on what we now call social determinants of Health. Consequently, WHO challenged political, academic, community, and professional organizations devoted to improving or preserving Health to make the scope of their work explicit, including their rationale for allocating resources.

Chapter 11. Neuman`s Systems Model in Nursing Practice,

Resources	A resource is any physical or virtual entity of limited availability, commercial or even ethic factors require resource allocation through resource management. As resources are very useful, we attach some information value to them.

Chapter 12. Orem`s Self-Care Deficit Theory in Nursing Practice,

Nursing	Nursing is a healthcare profession focused on the care of individuals, families, and communities so they may attain, maintain, or recover optimal health and quality of life from conception to death.
	Nurses work in a large variety of specialties where they work independently and as part of a team to assess, plan, implement and evaluate care. Nursing Science is a field of knowledge based on the contributions of nursing scientist through peer reviewed scholarly journals and evidenced-based practice.
Nursing Theory	Nursing theory is the term given to the body of knowledge that is used to define or explain various aspects of the profession of nursing.
	Types of nursing theories
	Grand nursing theories
	Grand nursing theories have the broadest scope and present general concepts and propositions. Theories at this level may both reflect and provide insights useful for practice but are not designed for empirical testing.
Self-Care Deficit Nursing Theory	The self-care deficit nursing theory is a grand nursing theory that was developed between 1959 and 2001 by Dorothea Orem. It is also known as the Orem model of nursing. It is particularly used in rehabilitation and primary care settings where the patient is encouraged to be as independent as possible.
Goal	Goal refers to a method of scoring in many sports. It can also refer to the physical structure or area of the playing surface in which a score is made.
	The structure of a Goal can vary widely from sport to sport.

Chapter 12. Orem`s Self-Care Deficit Theory in Nursing Practice,

Concept	A concept is a cognitive unit of meaning--an abstract idea or a mental symbol sometimes defined as a "unit of knowledge," built from other units which act as a concept's characteristics. A concept is typically associated with a corresponding representation in a language or symbology such as a single meaning of a term. There are prevailing theories in contemporary philosophy which attempt to explain the nature of concepts.
Knowledge	Knowledge is defined by the Oxford English Dictionary as (i) expertise, and skills acquired by a person through experience or education; the theoretical or practical understanding of a subject; (ii) what is known in a particular field or in total; facts and information; or (iii) be absolutely certain or sure about something. Philosophical debates in general start with Plato's formulation of knowledge as "justified true belief." There is however no single agreed definition of knowledge presently, nor any prospect of one, and there remain numerous competing theories. Knowledge acquisition involves complex cognitive processes: perception, learning, communication, association and reasoning.
Regulatory	Regulation refers to `controlling human or societal behaviour by rules or restrictions.` Regulation can take many forms: legal restrictions promulgated by a government authority, self-regulation, social regulation (e.g. norms), co-regulation and market regulation. One can consider regulation as actions of conduct imposing sanctions (such as a fine.) This action of administrative law, or implementing regulatory law, may be contrasted with statutory or case law.
Adherence	Adherence is often an essential step in bacterial pathogenesis or infection, required for colonizing a new host. To effectively adhere to host surfaces, many bacteria produce multiple Adherence factors called adhesins. For example, nontypeable Haemophilus influenzae expresses the adhesins Hia, Hap, Oap and a hemagglutinating pili.
Nursing diagnosis	A Nursing diagnosis is a standardized statement about the health of a client (who can be an individual, a family, or a community) for the purpose of providing nursing care. Nursing diagnoses are developed based on data obtained during the nursing assessment. The main organization for defining standard diagnoses in North America is the North American Nursing diagnosis Association, now known as NANDA-International.

Chapter 12. Orem`s Self-Care Deficit Theory in Nursing Practice,

Case study	A case study is a research method common in social science. It is based on an in-depth investigation of a single individual, group, or event. Case studies may be descriptive or explanatory.
Regimen	A regimen is a plan, a regulated course such as a diet, exercise or medical treatment, designed to give a positive result. A low-salt diet is a regimen. A course of penicillin is a regimen.
Healing	Physiological healing is the restoration of damaged living tissue to normal function. It is the process by which the cells in the body regenerate and repair to reduce the size of a damaged or necrotic area. Healing incorporates both the removal of necrotic tissue (demolition), and the replacement of this tissue.
Prevention	Prevention refers to:
	· Preventive medicine
	· Hazard Prevention, the process of risk study and elimination and mitigation in emergency management
	· Risk Prevention
	· Risk management
	· Preventive maintenance
	· Crime Prevention
	· Prevention, an album by Scottish band De Rosa
	· Prevention a magazine about health in the United States
	· Prevent (company), a textile company from Slovenia

Clam101

Chapter 12. Orem`s Self-Care Deficit Theory in Nursing Practice,

| Self-image | A person's self-image is the mental picture, generally of a kind that is quite resistant to change, that depicts not only details that are potentially available to objective investigation by others (height, weight, hair color, gender, I.Q. score, etc)., but also items that have been learned by that person about himself or herself, either from personal experiences or by internalizing the judgments of others. A simple definition of a person's self-image is their answer to this question - "What do you believe people think about you?" A more technical term for self-image that is commonly used by social and cognitive psychologists is self-schema. Like any schema, self-schemas store information and influence the way we think and remember. |

Chapter 13. Rogers` Science of Unitary Human Beings in Nursing Practice,

Humans	Humans commonly refers to the species Homo sapiens , the only extant member of the Homo genus of bipedal primates in Hominidae, the great ape family. However, in some cases the term is used to refer to any member of the genus Homo.
	Humans have a highly developed brain, capable of abstract reasoning, language, introspection, and problem solving.
Science of Unitary Human Beings	The science of unitary human beings is a grand nursing theory developed by Martha E. Rogers. The details of the theory are included in her book, An Introduction to the Theoretical Basis of Nursing.
	Overview
	According to Rogers, Nursing is both a science and an art.
Customer	A customer buyer, is usually used to refer to a current or potential buyer or user of the products of an individual or organization, called the supplier, seller, or vendor. This is typically through purchasing or renting goods or services. However, in certain contexts, the term customer also includes by extension anyone who uses or experiences the services of another.
Education	Education in the largest sense is any act or experience that has a formative effect on the mind, character or physical ability of an individual. In its technical sense, education is the process by which society deliberately transmits its accumulated knowledge, skills and values from one generation to another.
	Etymologically, the word education is derived from educare "bring up", which is related to educere "bring out", "bring forth what is within", "bring out potential" and ducere, "to lead".

187

Chapter 13. Rogers` Science of Unitary Human Beings in Nursing Practice,

Energy	Mental or psychic energy is the concept of a principle of activity powering the operation of the mind or psyche. Many modern psychologists or neuroscientists would equate it with increased metabolism in neurons of the brain. Philosophical accounts The idea harks back to Aristotle's conception of actus et potentia.
Health	At the time of the creation of the World Health Organization (WHO), in 1948, Health was defined as being `a state of complete physical, mental, and social well-being and not merely the absence of disease or infirmity`. This definition invited nations to expand the conceptual framework of their Health systems beyond issues related to the physical condition of individuals and their diseases, and it motivated us to focus our attention on what we now call social determinants of Health. Consequently, WHO challenged political, academic, community, and professional organizations devoted to improving or preserving Health to make the scope of their work explicit, including their rationale for allocating resources.
Openness	Openness is a very general philosophical position from which some individuals and organizations operate, often highlighted by a decision-making process recognizing communal management by distributed stakeholders (users/producers/contributors) rather than a centralized authority (owners, experts, boards of directors, etc). Openness could be a synonym of : .
Theory	Originally the word theory is a technical term from Ancient Greek. It is derived from theoria, θεωρ? α, meaning "a looking at, viewing, beholding", and refers to contemplation or speculation, as opposed to action. Theory is especially often contrasted to "practice" a concept that in its original Aristotelian context referred to actions done for their own sake, but can also refer to "technical" actions instrumental to some other aim, such as the making of tools or houses.

Chapter 13. Rogers` Science of Unitary Human Beings in Nursing Practice,

Healing	Physiological healing is the restoration of damaged living tissue to normal function. It is the process by which the cells in the body regenerate and repair to reduce the size of a damaged or necrotic area. Healing incorporates both the removal of necrotic tissue (demolition), and the replacement of this tissue.
Heart	The Heart is one of the zàng organs stipulated by Traditional Chinese Medicine (TCM). It is a functionally defined entity and not equivalent to the anatomical organ of the same name.
	In the context of the zang-fu concept
	As a zàng, the Heart is considered to be a yin organ.
Theories	[For a more detailed account of theories as expressed in formal language as they are studied in mathematical logic see Theory (mathematical logic.)]
	The term theory has two broad sets of meanings, one used in the empirical sciences (both natural and social) and the other used in philosophy, mathematics, logic, and across other fields in the humanities. There is considerable difference and even dispute across academic disciplines as to the proper usages of the term. What follows is an attempt to describe how the term is used, not to try to say how it ought to be used.
Adaptation	Adaptation is the process whereby a population becomes better suited to its habitat. This process takes place over many generations, and is one of the basic phenomena of biology.
	The significance of an Adaptation can only be understood in relation to the total biology of the species.
Communication	Communication is a process of transferring information from one entity to another. Communication processes are sign-mediated interactions between at least two agents which share a repertoire of signs and semiotic rules. Communication is commonly defined as `the imparting or interchange of thoughts, opinions, or information by speech, writing, or signs`.

Clam101

Chapter 13. Rogers' Science of Unitary Human Beings in Nursing Practice,

Regulatory	Regulation refers to 'controlling human or societal behaviour by rules or restrictions.' Regulation can take many forms: legal restrictions promulgated by a government authority, self-regulation, social regulation (e.g. norms), co-regulation and market regulation. One can consider regulation as actions of conduct imposing sanctions (such as a fine.) This action of administrative law, or implementing regulatory law, may be contrasted with statutory or case law.
Nursing	Nursing is a healthcare profession focused on the care of individuals, families, and communities so they may attain, maintain, or recover optimal health and quality of life from conception to death.
	Nurses work in a large variety of specialties where they work independently and as part of a team to assess, plan, implement and evaluate care. Nursing Science is a field of knowledge based on the contributions of nursing scientist through peer reviewed scholarly journals and evidenced-based practice.
Synthesis	In general, the noun Synthesis refers to the combining of two or more entities to form something new. The corresponding verb, to Synthesise , means to make or form a Synthesis.
	Synthesis or Synthesise may also refer to:
	· Chemical Synthesis, the execution of chemical reactions to form a more complex molecule from chemical precursors
	· Organic Synthesis, the chemical Synthesis of organic compounds
	· Total Synthesis, the complete organic Synthesis of complex organic compounds, usually without the aid of biological processes
	· Convergent Synthesis or linear Synthesis, a strategy to improve the efficiency of multi-step chemical syntheses

· Dehydration Synthesis, a chemical Synthesis resulting in the loss of a water molecule

· BioSynthesis, the creation of an organic compound in a living organism, usually aided by enzymes

· PhotoSynthesis, a biochemical reaction using a carbon molecule to produce an organic molecule, using sunlight as a catalyst

· ChemoSynthesis, the Synthesis of biological compounds into organic waste, using methane or an oxidized molecule as a catalyst

· Amino acid Synthesis, the Synthesis of an amino acid from its constituents*

· Peptide Synthesis, the biochemical Synthesis of peptides using amino acids

· Protein bioSynthesis, the multi-step biochemical Synthesis of proteins (long peptides)

· DNA Synthesis several biochemical processes for making DNA

· DNA replication, DNA bioSynthesis in vivo

· RNA Synthesis, the Synthesis of RNA from nucleic acids, using another nucleic acid chain as a template

· ATP Synthesis, the biochemical Synthesis of ATP

·

Chapter 13. Rogers` Science of Unitary Human Beings in Nursing Practice,

· [tyler wayne covington is the hottest motocrosser everrrrrr!]

· the process of converting a higher-level form of a design into a lower-level implementation

· Logic Synthesis

· High-level Synthesis

· Sound Synthesis, various methods of sound generation in audio electronics

· Subtractive Synthesis

· Frequency modulation Synthesis

· Speech Synthesis, the artificial production of human speech

· in philosophy, the end result of a dialectic, as in thesis, antithesis, Synthesis

· a cognitive skill in Benjamin Bloom`s Taxonomy of Educational Objectives.

· In philosophy and science, a higher a priori process than analysis

· Synthesis a web site and magazine covering popular culture

· Synthesis a journal of chemical Synthesis. .

Chapter 13. Rogers` Science of Unitary Human Beings in Nursing Practice,

Perspective	Perspective, in context of vision and visual perception, is the way in which objects appear to the eye based on their spatial attributes; or their dimensions and the position of the eye relative to the objects. There are two main meanings of the term: linear perspective and aerial perspective.
	Linear perspective
	As objects become more distant they appear smaller because their visual angle decreases.
Transformation	In molecular biology, transformation is the genetic alteration of a cell resulting from the uptake, genomic incorporation, and expression of environmental genetic material (DNA). Transformation ransformation occurs most commonly in bacteria, both naturally and artificially, and refers to DNA taken up from the environment through their cell wall. Bacteria that are capable of being transformed are called competent.
Disease	A disease is an abnormal condition affecting the body of an organism. It is often construed to be a medical condition associated with specific symptoms and signs. It may be caused by external factors, such as infectious disease, or it may be caused by internal dysfunctions, such as autoimmune diseases.
Case study	A case study is a research method common in social science. It is based on an in-depth investigation of a single individual, group, or event. Case studies may be descriptive or explanatory.
Fear	Fear is a distressing emotion aroused by a perceived threat. It is a basic survival mechanism occurring in response to a specific stimulus, such as pain or the threat of danger. In short, fear is the ability to recognize danger and flee from it or confront it, also known as the Fight or Flight response.
Pain	Pain is "an unpleasant sensory and emotional experience associated with actual or potential tissue damage, or described in terms of such damage." It is the feeling common to such experiences as stubbing a toe, burning a finger, putting iodine on a cut, and bumping the "funny bone".

	Pain motivates us to withdraw from potentially damaging situations, protect a damaged body part while it heals, and avoid those situations in the future. Most pain resolves promptly once the painful stimulus is removed and the body has healed, but sometimes pain persists despite removal of the stimulus and apparent healing of the body; and sometimes pain arises in the absence of any detectable stimulus, damage or disease.
Pain assessment	Pain is often regarded as the fifth vital sign in regards to healthcare because it is accepted now in healthcare that pain, like other vital signs, is an objective sensation rather than subjective. As a result nurses are trained and expected to assess pain. Regulation Pain assessment and re-assessment after administration of analgesics or pain management is regulated in healthcare facilities by accreditation bodies, like the Joint Commission.
Surgery	Surgery is an ancient medical specialty that uses operative manual and instrumental techniques on a patient to investigate and/or treat a pathological condition such as disease or injury, to help improve bodily function or appearance, and sometimes for religious reasons. An act of performing surgery may be called a surgical procedure, operation, or simply surgery. In this context, the verb operate means performing surgery.
Intention	An agent's intention in performing an action is his or her specific purpose in doing so, the end or goal that is aimed at, or intended to accomplish. Whether an action is successful or unsuccessful depends at least on whether the intended result was brought about. Other consequences of someone's acting are called unintentional.
Therapeutic	Therapy is the attempted remediation of a health problem, usually following a diagnosis. In the medical field, it is synonymous with the word `treatment`. A therapeutic effect is a consequence of a particular treatment which is judged to be desirable and beneficial.

Chapter 13. Rogers' Science of Unitary Human Beings in Nursing Practice,

Touch	The somatosensory system is a diverse sensory system comprising the receptors and processing centres to produce the sensory modalities such as touch, temperature, proprioception (body position), and nociception (pain). The sensory receptors cover the skin and epithelia, skeletal muscles, bones and joints, internal organs, and the cardiovascular system. While touch is considered one of the five traditional senses, the impression of touch is formed from several modalities; In medicine, the colloquial term touch is usually replaced with somatic senses to better reflect the variety of mechanisms involved.
Burn	A burn is a type of injury to flesh caused by heat, electricity, chemicals, light, radiation or friction. Most burns only affect the skin (epidermal tissue and dermis). Rarely, deeper tissues, such as muscle, bone, and blood vessels can also be injured.
Cancer	Cancer (medical term: malignant neoplasm) is a class of diseases in which a group of cells display uncontrolled growth, invasion that intrudes upon and destroys adjacent tissues, and sometimes metastasis, or spreading to other locations in the body via lymph or blood. These three malignant properties of cancers differentiate them from benign tumors, which do not invade or metastasize. Researchers divide the causes of cancer into two groups: those with an environmental cause and those with a hereditary genetic cause.
Data collection	Data collection is a term used to describe a process of preparing and collecting data - for example as part of a process improvement or similar project. The purpose of data collection is to obtain information to keep on record, to make decisions about important issues, to pass information on to others. Primarily, data is collected to provide information regarding a specific topic.
Image	An image is an artifact, for example a two-dimensional picture, that has a similar appearance to some subject--usually a physical object or a person. Characteristics

	Images may be two-dimensional, such as a photograph, screen display, and as well as a three-dimensional, such as a statue or hologram. They may be captured by optical devices--such as cameras, mirrors, lenses, telescopes, microscopes, etc.
Visible light	The visible spectrum is the portion of the electromagnetic spectrum that is visible to (can be detected by) the human eye. Electromagnetic radiation in this range of wavelengths is called Visible light or simply light. A typical human eye will respond to wavelengths from about 380 to 750 nm.
Therapeutic touch	Therapeutic touch (commonly shortened to),) or Distance Healing, is an energy therapy claimed to promote healing and reduce pain and anxiety. Practitioners of Therapeutic touch claim that by placing their hands on, or near, a patient, they are able to detect and manipulate the patient`s putative energy field. Although there are currently (September 2009) 259 articles concerning Therapeutic touch on PubMed the quality of controlled research and tests is variable.
Management	Management in all business and organizational activities is the act of getting people together to accomplish desired goals and objectives using available resources efficiently and effectively. Management comprises planning, organizing, staffing, leading or directing, and controlling an organization (a group of one or more people or entities) or effort for the purpose of accomplishing a goal. Resourcing encompasses the deployment and manipulation of human resources, financial resources, technological resources, and natural resources.
Medication	A pharmaceutical drug, also referred to as medicine, medication or medicament, can be loosely defined as any chemical substance intended for use in the medical diagnosis, cure, treatment, or prevention of disease.
	medications can be classified in various ways, such as by chemical properties, mode or route of administration, biological system affected, or therapeutic effects. An elaborate and widely used classification system is the Anatomical Therapeutic Chemical Classification System (ATC system).

Chapter 14. Roy`s Adaptation Model in Nursing Practice,

Adaptation	Adaptation is the process whereby a population becomes better suited to its habitat. This process takes place over many generations, and is one of the basic phenomena of biology.
	The significance of an Adaptation can only be understood in relation to the total biology of the species.
Healing	Physiological healing is the restoration of damaged living tissue to normal function. It is the process by which the cells in the body regenerate and repair to reduce the size of a damaged or necrotic area. Healing incorporates both the removal of necrotic tissue (demolition), and the replacement of this tissue.
Diagnosis	Diagnosis is the identification of the nature and cause of anything. Diagnosis is used in many different disciplines with variations in the use of logics, analytics, and experience to determine the cause and effect relationships. In systems engineering and computer science, diagnosis is typically used to determine the causes of symptoms, mitigations for problems, and solutions to issues.
Empathy	Empathy is the capacity to recognize and, to some extent, share feelings (such as sadness or happiness) that are being experienced by another semi-sentient being. Someone may need to have a certain amount of empathy before they are able to feel compassion.
	Etymology
	The English word is derived from the Greek word ?μπ?θεια (empatheia), "physical affection, passion, partiality" which comes from ?v (en), "in, at" + π?θος (pathos), "passion" or "suffering".
Health	At the time of the creation of the World Health Organization (WHO), in 1948, Health was defined as being `a state of complete physical, mental, and social well-being and not merely the absence of disease or infirmity`.
	This definition invited nations to expand the conceptual framework of their Health systems beyond issues related to the physical condition of individuals and their diseases, and it motivated us to focus our attention on what we now call social determinants of Health. Consequently, WHO challenged political, academic, community, and professional organizations devoted to improving or preserving Health to make the scope of their work explicit, including their rationale for allocating resources.

Chapter 14. Roy's Adaptation Model in Nursing Practice,

Humans	Humans commonly refers to the species Homo sapiens , the only extant member of the Homo genus of bipedal primates in Hominidae, the great ape family. However, in some cases the term is used to refer to any member of the genus Homo.
	Humans have a highly developed brain, capable of abstract reasoning, language, introspection, and problem solving.
Nursing	Nursing is a healthcare profession focused on the care of individuals, families, and communities so they may attain, maintain, or recover optimal health and quality of life from conception to death.
	Nurses work in a large variety of specialties where they work independently and as part of a team to assess, plan, implement and evaluate care. Nursing Science is a field of knowledge based on the contributions of nursing scientist through peer reviewed scholarly journals and evidenced-based practice.
Nursing Theory	Nursing theory is the term given to the body of knowledge that is used to define or explain various aspects of the profession of nursing.
	Types of nursing theories
	Grand nursing theories
	Grand nursing theories have the broadest scope and present general concepts and propositions. Theories at this level may both reflect and provide insights useful for practice but are not designed for empirical testing.
Nutrition	Nutrition is the provision, to cells and organisms, of the materials necessary (in the form of food) to support life. Many common health problems can be prevented or alleviated with a healthy diet.
	Overview

	Nutrition science investigates the metabolic and physiological responses of the body to diet.
Oxygenation	Oxygenation occurs when oxygen molecules (O_2) enter the tissues of the body. For example, blood is oxygenated in the lungs, where oxygen molecules travel from the air and into the blood. As a result of this oxygenation, the color of the blood changes from dark purple to red.
Regulatory	Regulation refers to `controlling human or societal behaviour by rules or restrictions.` Regulation can take many forms: legal restrictions promulgated by a government authority, self-regulation, social regulation (e.g. norms), co-regulation and market regulation. One can consider regulation as actions of conduct imposing sanctions (such as a fine.) This action of administrative law, or implementing regulatory law, may be contrasted with statutory or case law.
Science of Unitary Human Beings	The science of unitary human beings is a grand nursing theory developed by Martha E. Rogers. The details of the theory are included in her book, An Introduction to the Theoretical Basis of Nursing. Overview According to Rogers, Nursing is both a science and an art.
Self-Care Deficit Nursing Theory	The self-care deficit nursing theory is a grand nursing theory that was developed between 1959 and 2001 by Dorothea Orem. It is also known as the Orem model of nursing. It is particularly used in rehabilitation and primary care settings where the patient is encouraged to be as independent as possible.
Clinic	A Clinic is a small private or public health facility that is devoted to the care of outpatients, often in a community, in contrast to larger hospitals, which also treat inpatients. Some grow to be institutions as large as major hospitals, whilst retaining the name Clinic. These are often associated with a hospital or medical school.

Chapter 14. Roy`s Adaptation Model in Nursing Practice,

Role	A Role or a social Role is a set of connected behaviors, rights and obligations as conceptualized by actors in a social situation. It is an expected or free or continously changing behavior and may have a given individual social status or social position. It is vital to both functionalist and interactionist understandings of society. Social Role posits the following about social behavior:
	· The division of labor in society takes the form of the interaction among heterogeneous specialized positions, we call Roles.
	· Social Roles included appropriate and permitted forms of behavior, guided by social norms, which are commonly known and hence determine the expectations for appropriate behavior in these Roles.
	· Roles are occupied by individuals, who are called actors.
	· When individuals approve of a social Role (i.e., they consider the Role legitimate and constructive, they will incur costs to conform to Role norms, and will also incur costs to punish those who violate Role norms.
	· Changed conditions can render a social Role outdated or illegitimate, in which case social pressures are likely to lead to Role change.
	· The anticipation of rewards and punishments, as well as the satisfaction of behaving prosocially, account for why agents conform to Role requirmeets.
Assessment	Educational Assessment is the process of documenting, usually in measurable terms, knowledge, skills, attitudes and beliefs. Assessment can focus on the individual learner, the learning community (class, workshop, or other organized group of learners), the institution, or the educational system as a whole. According to the Academic Exchange Quarterly: 'Studies of a theoretical or empirical nature addressing the Assessment of learner aptitude and preparation, motivation and learning styles, learning outcomes in achievement and satisfaction in different educational contexts are all welcome, as are studies addressing issues of measurable standards and benchmarks'.
Nursing diagnosis	A Nursing diagnosis is a standardized statement about the health of a client (who can be an individual, a family, or a community) for the purpose of providing nursing care. Nursing diagnoses are developed based on data obtained during the nursing assessment.

Chapter 14. Roy`s Adaptation Model in Nursing Practice,

	The main organization for defining standard diagnoses in North America is the North American Nursing diagnosis Association, now known as NANDA-International.
Case study	A case study is a research method common in social science. It is based on an in-depth investigation of a single individual, group, or event. Case studies may be descriptive or explanatory.
Physiology	Physiology is the science of the function of living systems. It is a subcategory of biology. In physiology, the scientific method is applied to determine how organisms, organ systems, organs, cells and biomolecules carry out the chemical or physical function that they have in a living system. Human physiology is the science of the mechanical, physical, and biochemical functions of humans in good health, their organs, and the cells of which they are composed. The principal level of focus of physiology is at the level of organs and systems within systems. Much of the foundation of knowledge in human physiology was provided by animal experimentation. Physiology is closely related to anatomy; anatomy is the study of form, and physiology is the study of function. Due to the frequent connection between form and function physiology and anatomy are intrinsically linked and are studied in tandem as part of a medical curriculum.
Amotivational syndrome	Amotivational syndrome is a syndrome associated with diminished inspiration to participate in normal social situations and activities, with lapses in apathy caused by an external event, situation, substance, relationship, and that persons who fit the definition are normal, if introverted humans, and that such people tend to enjoy smoking cannabis because it reinforces this behavior.
AIDS	AIDS is a peer-reviewed scientific journal that is published by Lippincott Williams ' Wilkins (London, United Kingdom). It was established in 1987 and is the official journal of the International AIDS Society. It covers all aspects of HIV and AIDS, including basic science, clinical trials, epidemiology, and social science.
Acquired disorder	An acquired disorder is a medical condition which develops post-fetally; in contrast with a congenital disorder, which is present at birth. A congenital disorder may be antecedent to an acquired disorder. The term acquired may also be used to describe permanent or temporary modifications or devices (such as a shunt) which have been placed or created by a medical professional during palliation or treatment of a medical condition.

Chapter 14. Roy`s Adaptation Model in Nursing Practice,

Immunodeficiency	Immunodeficiency is a state in which the immune system`s ability to fight infectious disease is compromised or entirely absent. Most cases of Immunodeficiency are acquired (`secondary`) but some people are born with defects in the immune system, or primary Immunodeficiency. Transplant patients take medications to suppress their immune system as an anti-rejection measure, as do some patients suffering from an over-active immune system.
Syndrome	In medicine and psychology, a syndrome is the association of several clinically recognizable features, signs (observed by a physician), symptoms (reported by the patient), phenomena or characteristics that often occur together, so that the presence of one or more features alerts the physician to the possible presence of the others. Specific syndromes tend to have a range of possible etiologies or diseases that could create such a set of circumstances. I.e.
Spiritual distress	Spiritual distress is a disturbance in a person`s belief system. As an approved nursing diagnosis, Spiritual distress is defined as `a disruption in the life principle that pervades a person`s entire being and that integrates and transcends one`s biological and psychological nature.` Authors in the field of nursing who contributed to the definition of the characteristics of Spiritual distress used indicators to validate diagnoses. The following manifestations of Spiritual distress are a part of an abstract data gathered by LearnWell Resources, Inc from the studies of Mary Elizabeth O`Brien and is used as a Spiritual Assessment Guide to present alterations in spiritual integrity.
Fear	Fear is a distressing emotion aroused by a perceived threat. It is a basic survival mechanism occurring in response to a specific stimulus, such as pain or the threat of danger. In short, fear is the ability to recognize danger and flee from it or confront it, also known as the Fight or Flight response.

Chapter 15. Orlando`s Nursing Process Theory in Nursing Practice,

Nursing	Nursing is a healthcare profession focused on the care of individuals, families, and communities so they may attain, maintain, or recover optimal health and quality of life from conception to death. Nurses work in a large variety of specialties where they work independently and as part of a team to assess, plan, implement and evaluate care. Nursing Science is a field of knowledge based on the contributions of nursing scientist through peer reviewed scholarly journals and evidenced-based practice.
Nursing Process	The nursing process is a process by which nurses deliver care to individuals, families, and/or communities and is supported by nursing theories. The nursing process was originally an adapted form of problem-solving and is classified as a deductive theory. Phases of the nursing process The nursing process is a client-centered, goal-oriented method of caring that provides a framework to nursing care.
Theory	Originally the word theory is a technical term from Ancient Greek. It is derived from theoria, θεωρ? α, meaning "a looking at, viewing, beholding", and refers to contemplation or speculation, as opposed to action. Theory is especially often contrasted to "practice" a concept that in its original Aristotelian context referred to actions done for their own sake, but can also refer to "technical" actions instrumental to some other aim, such as the making of tools or houses.
Assessment	Educational Assessment is the process of documenting, usually in measurable terms, knowledge, skills, attitudes and beliefs. Assessment can focus on the individual learner, the learning community (class, workshop, or other organized group of learners), the institution, or the educational system as a whole. According to the Academic Exchange Quarterly: 'Studies of a theoretical or empirical nature addressing the Assessment of learner aptitude and preparation, motivation and learning styles, learning outcomes in achievement and satisfaction in different educational contexts are all welcome, as are studies addressing issues of measurable standards and benchmarks'.

Chapter 15. Orlando`s Nursing Process Theory in Nursing Practice,

Immediate	Immediate Records was a British record label, started in 1965 by The Rolling Stones manager Andrew Loog Oldham and Tony Calder concentrating on the London-based blues and R'B scene. Signed musicians included Rod Stewart, P. P. Arnold, Billy Nicholls, John Mayall, Savoy Brown, Small Faces, The Nice, Fleetwood Mac, The Groundhogs, Chris Farlowe, Duncan Browne and Humble Pie. There is evidence of recordings of two Mike d'Abo songs 'Little Miss Understood' and 'So Much to Say (So Little Time)' from The immediate Singles Collection (1985; CCSCD 102), a compilation of immediate Record's hits (including the rare cut 'Someone's Gonna Get Their Head Kicked in Tonite' [sic] by the Jeremy Spencer-fronted configuration Earl Vince and the Valiants.
Nutrition	Nutrition is the provision, to cells and organisms, of the materials necessary (in the form of food) to support life. Many common health problems can be prevented or alleviated with a healthy diet. Overview Nutrition science investigates the metabolic and physiological responses of the body to diet.
Perception	In philosophy, psychology, and cognitive science, perception is the process of attaining awareness or understanding of sensory information. The word "perception" comes from the Latin words perceptio, percipio, and means "receiving, collecting, action of taking possession, apprehension with the mind or senses." Perception is one of the oldest fields in psychology. The oldest quantitative law in psychology is the Weber-Fechner law, which quantifies the relationship between the intensity of physical stimuli and their perceptual effects.
Nurse	A Nurse is a healthcare professional who, in collaboration with other members of a health care team, is responsible for: treatment, safety, and recovery of acutely or chronically ill individuals; health promotion and maintenance within families, communities and populations; and, treatment of life-threatening emergencies in a wide range of health care settings. Nurses perform a wide range of clinical and non-clinical functions necessary to the delivery of health care, and may also be involved in medical and nursing research.

CtamlOI

Chapter 15. Orlando`s Nursing Process Theory in Nursing Practice,

	Both Nursing roles and education were first defined by Florence Nightingale, following her experiences caring for the wounded in the Crimean War.
Concept	A concept is a cognitive unit of meaning--an abstract idea or a mental symbol sometimes defined as a "unit of knowledge," built from other units which act as a concept's characteristics. A concept is typically associated with a corresponding representation in a language or symbology such as a single meaning of a term.
	There are prevailing theories in contemporary philosophy which attempt to explain the nature of concepts.
Nursing Theory	Nursing theory is the term given to the body of knowledge that is used to define or explain various aspects of the profession of nursing.
	Types of nursing theories
	Grand nursing theories
	Grand nursing theories have the broadest scope and present general concepts and propositions. Theories at this level may both reflect and provide insights useful for practice but are not designed for empirical testing.
Self-Care Deficit Nursing Theory	The self-care deficit nursing theory is a grand nursing theory that was developed between 1959 and 2001 by Dorothea Orem. It is also known as the Orem model of nursing. It is particularly used in rehabilitation and primary care settings where the patient is encouraged to be as independent as possible.
Case study	A case study is a research method common in social science. It is based on an in-depth investigation of a single individual, group, or event. Case studies may be descriptive or explanatory.

Chapter 15. Orlando`s Nursing Process Theory in Nursing Practice,

Tuberculosis	Tuberculosis, MTB or TB (short for tubercles bacillus) is a common and in some cases deadly infectious disease caused by various strains of mycobacteria, usually Mycobacterium tuberculosis in humans. Tuberculosis usually attacks the lungs but can also affect other parts of the body. It is spread through the air when people who have active MTB infection cough, sneeze, or spit.

Chapter 16. Modeling and Role-Modeling Theory in Nursing Practice,

Theory	Originally the word theory is a technical term from Ancient Greek. It is derived from theoria, θεωρ? α, meaning "a looking at, viewing, beholding", and refers to contemplation or speculation, as opposed to action. Theory is especially often contrasted to "practice" a concept that in its original Aristotelian context referred to actions done for their own sake, but can also refer to "technical" actions instrumental to some other aim, such as the making of tools or houses.
Assessment	Educational Assessment is the process of documenting, usually in measurable terms, knowledge, skills, attitudes and beliefs. Assessment can focus on the individual learner, the learning community (class, workshop, or other organized group of learners), the institution, or the educational system as a whole. According to the Academic Exchange Quarterly: 'Studies of a theoretical or empirical nature addressing the Assessment of learner aptitude and preparation, motivation and learning styles, learning outcomes in achievement and satisfaction in different educational contexts are all welcome, as are studies addressing issues of measurable standards and benchmarks'.
Nursing	Nursing is a healthcare profession focused on the care of individuals, families, and communities so they may attain, maintain, or recover optimal health and quality of life from conception to death.
	Nurses work in a large variety of specialties where they work independently and as part of a team to assess, plan, implement and evaluate care. Nursing Science is a field of knowledge based on the contributions of nursing scientist through peer reviewed scholarly journals and evidenced-based practice.
Paradigm	The word paradigm has been used in science to describe distinct concepts. It comes from Greek "παρ?δειγμα" (paradeigma), "pattern, example, sample" from the verb "παραδε? κνυμι" (paradeiknumi), "exhibit, represent, expose" and that from "παρ?" (para), "beside, by" + "δε?κνυμι" (deiknumi), "to show, to point out".
	The original Greek term παραδε?γματι (paradeigma) was used in Greek texts such as Plato's Timaeus (28A) as the model or the pattern that the Demiurge (god) used to create the cosmos.
Telerobotics	Telerobotics is the area of robotics concerned with the control of robots from a distance, chiefly using wireless connections (like Wi-Fi, Bluetooth, the Deep Space Network, and similar), `tethered` connections, teleoperation and telepresence.

227

Chapter 16. Modeling and Role-Modeling Theory in Nursing Practice,

	Teleoperation means `doing work at a distance`, although `work` may mean almost anything.
Cognition	Cognition is the scientific term for "the process of thought". Usage of the term varies in different disciplines; for example in psychology and cognitive science, it usually refers to an information processing view of an individual's psychological functions. Other interpretations of the meaning of cognition link it to the development of concepts; individual minds, groups, and organizations.
Genetic predisposition	A Genetic predisposition is a genetic affectation which influences the phenotype of an individual organism within a species or population but by definition that phenotype can also be modified by the environmental conditions. In the rest of the population, conditions cannot have that affect. Genetic testing is able to identify individuals who are genetically predisposed to certain health problems.
Goal	Goal refers to a method of scoring in many sports. It can also refer to the physical structure or area of the playing surface in which a score is made. The structure of a Goal can vary widely from sport to sport.
Humans	Humans commonly refers to the species Homo sapiens , the only extant member of the Homo genus of bipedal primates in Hominidae, the great ape family. However, in some cases the term is used to refer to any member of the genus Homo. Humans have a highly developed brain, capable of abstract reasoning, language, introspection, and problem solving.
Resources	A resource is any physical or virtual entity of limited availability, commercial or even ethic factors require resource allocation through resource management. As resources are very useful, we attach some information value to them.

Chapter 16. Modeling and Role-Modeling Theory in Nursing Practice,

Knowledge	Knowledge is defined by the Oxford English Dictionary as (i) expertise, and skills acquired by a person through experience or education; the theoretical or practical understanding of a subject; (ii) what is known in a particular field or in total; facts and information; or (iii) be absolutely certain or sure about something. Philosophical debates in general start with Plato's formulation of knowledge as "justified true belief." There is however no single agreed definition of knowledge presently, nor any prospect of one, and there remain numerous competing theories. Knowledge acquisition involves complex cognitive processes: perception, learning, communication, association and reasoning.
Process and Reality	In philosophy, especially metaphysics, the book Process and Reality by Alfred North Whitehead sets out its author's philosophy of organism published in 1929, is a revision of the Gifford Lectures he gave in 1927-28. Process philosophy lays the groundwork for a paradigm of subjectivity, which Whitehead calls a `completed metaphysical language.` (p.
Nursing Process	The nursing process is a process by which nurses deliver care to individuals, families, and/or communities and is supported by nursing theories. The nursing process was originally an adapted form of problem-solving and is classified as a deductive theory. Phases of the nursing process The nursing process is a client-centered, goal-oriented method of caring that provides a framework to nursing care.
Caregiver	Carer (UK, NZ, Australian usage) and Caregiver are words normally used to refer to unpaid relatives or friends who support people with disabilities. The words may be prefixed with `family` `spousal`, `child` to distinguish between different care situations. The general term dependent/dependant care is also used for the service provided.
Stress	Stress is a term in psychology and biology, first coined in the biological context in the 1930s, which has in more recent decades become commonly used in popular parlance. It refers to the consequence of the failure of an organism - human or animal - to respond appropriately to emotional or physical threats, whether actual or imagined.

Chapter 16. Modeling and Role-Modeling Theory in Nursing Practice,

	Signs of stress may be cognitive, emotional, physical or behavioral.
Stress Response	The `fight-or-flight response` the `fright, fight or flight response`, `hyperarousal` or the `acute stress response`, was first described by Walter Cannon in 1929. His theory states that animals react to threats with a general discharge of the sympathetic nervous system, priming the animal for fighting or fleeing. This response was later recognized as the first stage of a general adaptation syndrome that regulates stress response s among vertebrates and other organisms.
Acute	In medicine, an acute disease is a disease with either or both of: 1. a rapid onset, as in acute infection 2. a short course (as opposed to a chronic course). This adjective is part of the definition of several diseases and is, therefore, incorporated in their name, for instance, severe acute respiratory syndrome, acute leukemia. The term acute may often be confused by the general public to mean 'severe'. This however, is a different characteristic and something can be acute but not severe.
Communication	Communication is a process of transferring information from one entity to another. Communication processes are sign-mediated interactions between at least two agents which share a repertoire of signs and semiotic rules. Communication is commonly defined as `the imparting or interchange of thoughts, opinions, or information by speech, writing, or signs`.
Grief	Grief is a multi-faceted response to loss, particularly to the loss of someone or something to which a bond was formed. Although conventionally focused on the emotional response to loss, it also has physical, cognitive, behavioral, social, and philosophical dimensions. While the terms are often used interchangeably, bereavement often refers to the state of loss, and grief to the reaction to loss.
Case study	A case study is a research method common in social science. It is based on an in-depth investigation of a single individual, group, or event. Case studies may be descriptive or explanatory.

Chapter 16. Modeling and Role-Modeling Theory in Nursing Practice,

Description	Description is one of four rhetorical modes (also known as modes of discourse), along with exposition, argumentation, and narration. Each of the rhetorical modes is present in a variety of forms and each has its own purpose and conventions. Description is also the fiction-writing mode for transmitting a mental image of the particulars of a story.
Impression	A dental impression may be described as an accurate representation of part or all of a person's dentition and other areas of the mouth. The dental impression forms an imprint (i.e. a 'negative' mould) of those teeth and gums, which can then be used to make a cast or 'positive' model of the dentition. This may be used for the fabrication of dentures, crowns or other prostheses.
Nursing home	A Nursing home, convalescent home, Skilled Nursing Unit (SNU), care home or rest home provides a type of care of residents: it is a place of residence for people who require constant nursing care and have significant deficiencies with activities of daily living. Residents include the elderly and younger adults with physical or mental disabilities. Eligible adults 18 or older can stay in a skilled nursing facility to receive physical, occupational, and other rehabilitative therapies following an accident or illness.

Chapter 17. Mercer's Becoming a Mother Theory in Nursing Practice,

Experience	Experience as a general concept comprises knowledge of or skill in or observation of some thing or some event gained through involvement in or exposure to that thing or event. The history of the word experience aligns it closely with the concept of experiment.
	The concept of experience generally refers to know-how or procedural knowledge, rather than propositional knowledge: on-the-job training rather than book-learning.
Humans	Humans commonly refers to the species Homo sapiens , the only extant member of the Homo genus of bipedal primates in Hominidae, the great ape family. However, in some cases the term is used to refer to any member of the genus Homo.
	Humans have a highly developed brain, capable of abstract reasoning, language, introspection, and problem solving.
Role	A Role or a social Role is a set of connected behaviors, rights and obligations as conceptualized by actors in a social situation. It is an expected or free or continously changing behavior and may have a given individual social status or social position. It is vital to both functionalist and interactionist understandings of society. Social Role posits the following about social behavior:
	· The division of labor in society takes the form of the interaction among heterogeneous specialized positions, we call Roles.
	· Social Roles included appropriate and permitted forms of behavior, guided by social norms, which are commonly known and hence determine the expectations for appropriate behavior in these Roles.
	· Roles are occupied by individuals, who are called actors.
	· When individuals approve of a social Role (i.e., they consider the Role legitimate and constructive, they will incur costs to conform to Role norms, and will also incur costs to punish those who violate Role norms.
	· Changed conditions can render a social Role outdated or illegitimate, in which case social pressures are likely to lead to Role change.

Chapter 17. Mercer`s Becoming a Mother Theory in Nursing Practice,

	· The anticipation of rewards and punishments, as well as the satisfaction of behaving prosocially, account for why agents conform to Role requirmeets.
Theory	Originally the word theory is a technical term from Ancient Greek. It is derived from theoria, θεωρ? α, meaning "a looking at, viewing, beholding", and refers to contemplation or speculation, as opposed to action. Theory is especially often contrasted to "practice" a concept that in its original Aristotelian context referred to actions done for their own sake, but can also refer to "technical" actions instrumental to some other aim, such as the making of tools or houses.
Family	Family is a group of people or animals (many species form the equivalent of a human Family wherein the adults care for the young) affiliated by consanguinity, affinity or co-residence. Although the concept of consanguinity originally referred to relations by `blood`, anthropologists have argued that one must understand the idea of `blood` metaphorically and that many societies understand Family through other concepts rather than through genetic distance. One of the primary functions of the Family is to produce and reproduce persons, biologically and socially.
Family therapy	Family therapy, also referred to as couple and family therapy and family systems therapy, is a branch of psychotherapy that works with families and couples in intimate relationships to nurture change and development. It tends to view change in terms of the systems of interaction between family members. It emphasizes family relationships as an important factor in psychological health.
Assessment	Educational Assessment is the process of documenting, usually in measurable terms, knowledge, skills, attitudes and beliefs. Assessment can focus on the individual learner, the learning community (class, workshop, or other organized group of learners), the institution, or the educational system as a whole. According to the Academic Exchange Quarterly: 'Studies of a theoretical or empirical nature addressing the Assessment of learner aptitude and preparation, motivation and learning styles, learning outcomes in achievement and satisfaction in different educational contexts are all welcome, as are studies addressing issues of measurable standards and benchmarks'.
Nursing	Nursing is a healthcare profession focused on the care of individuals, families, and communities so they may attain, maintain, or recover optimal health and quality of life from conception to death.

Chapter 17. Mercer's Becoming a Mother Theory in Nursing Practice,

Nurses work in a large variety of specialties where they work independently and as part of a team to assess, plan, implement and evaluate care. Nursing Science is a field of knowledge based on the contributions of nursing scientist through peer reviewed scholarly journals and evidenced-based practice.

Amotivational syndrome

Amotivational syndrome is a syndrome associated with diminished inspiration to participate in normal social situations and activities, with lapses in apathy caused by an external event, situation, substance, relationship, and that persons who fit the definition are normal, if introverted humans, and that such people tend to enjoy smoking cannabis because it reinforces this behavior.

Healing

Physiological healing is the restoration of damaged living tissue to normal function. It is the process by which the cells in the body regenerate and repair to reduce the size of a damaged or necrotic area. Healing incorporates both the removal of necrotic tissue (demolition), and the replacement of this tissue.

Orthopedic

Orthopedic surgery or Orthopedics (also spelled orthopaedics) is the branch of surgery concerned with conditions involving the musculoskeletal system. Orthopedic surgeons use both surgical and non-surgical means to treat musculoskeletal trauma, sports injuries, degenerative diseases, infections, tumors, and congenital conditions.

Nicholas Andry coined the word `orthopaedics`, derived from Greek words for orthos and paideion (`child`), when he published Orthopaedia: or the Art of Correcting and Preventing Deformities in Children in 1741.

Osteoporosis

Osteoporosis is a disease of bone that leads to an increased risk of fracture. In Osteoporosis the bone mineral density (BMD) is reduced, bone microarchitecture is disrupted, and the amount and variety of non-collagenous proteins in bone is altered. Osteoporosis is defined by the World Health Organization (WHO) in women as a bone mineral density 2.5 standard deviations below peak bone mass (20-year-old healthy female average) as measured by DXA; the term `established Osteoporosis` includes the presence of a fragility fracture.

Chapter 17. Mercer's Becoming a Mother Theory in Nursing Practice,

Outcome	In game theory, an outcome is a set of moves or strategies taken by the players, or their payoffs resulting from the actions or strategies taken by all players. The two are complementary in that, given knowledge of the set of strategies of all players, the final state of the game is known, as are any relevant payoffs. In a game where chance or a random event is involved, the outcome is not known from only the set of strategies, but is only realized when the random event(s) are realized.
Resources	A resource is any physical or virtual entity of limited availability, commercial or even ethic factors require resource allocation through resource management.
	As resources are very useful, we attach some information value to them.
Nursing theory	Nursing theory is the term given to the body of knowledge that is used to define or explain various aspects of the profession of nursing.
	Types of nursing theories
	Grand nursing theories
	Grand nursing theories have the broadest scope and present general concepts and propositions. Theories at this level may both reflect and provide insights useful for practice but are not designed for empirical testing.
Nipple	In its most general form, a Nipple is a structure from which a fluid emanates. More specifically, it is the projection on the breasts of a mammal by which breast milk is delivered to a mother's young.
	In the anatomy of mammals, a Nipple or mammary papilla or teat is a small projection of skin containing the outlets for 15-20 lactiferous ducts arranged cylindrically around the tip.
Urinary	The urinary system is the organ system that produces, stores, and eliminates urine. In humans it includes two kidneys, two ureters, the bladder, the urethra, and the penis in males. The analogous organ in invertebrates is the nephridium.

Chapter 17. Mercer's Becoming a Mother Theory in Nursing Practice,

Urinary tract infection	Urinary tract infection is a bacterial infection that affects any part of the urinary tract. Symptoms include frequent feeling and/or need to urinate, pain during urination, and cloudy urine. The main causal agent is Escherichia coli.
Individual	As commonly used, an Individual is a person or any specific object in a collection. In the 15th century and earlier, and also today within the fields of statistics and metaphysics, Individual means 'indivisible', typically describing any numerically singular thing, but sometimes meaning 'a person.' (q.v. 'The problem of proper names'). From the seventeenth century on, Individual indicates separateness, as in Individualism.
Neonatal intensive care unit	A neonatal intensive care unit, usually shortened neonatal intensive care unit and also called a newborn intensive care unit, intensive care nursery , and special care baby unit , is a unit of a hospital specializing in the care of ill or premature newborn infants. The neonatal intensive care unit is distinct from a special care nursery (SCN) in providing a high level of intensive care to premature infants while the SCN provides specialized care for infants with less severe medical problems. neonatal intensive care units were developed in the 1950s and 1960s by pediatricians to provide better temperature support, isolation from infection risk, specialized feeding, and greater access to specialized equipment and resources.
Pressure	Example reading: $1\ Pa = 1\ N/m^2 = 10^{-5}\ bar = 10.197 \times 10^{-6}\ at = 9.8692 \times 10^{-6}\ atm$, etc. As an example of varying Pressures, a finger can be pressed against a wall without making any lasting impression; however, the same finger pushing a thumbtack can easily damage the wall. Although the force applied to the surface is the same, the thumbtack applies more Pressure because the point concentrates that force into a smaller area.
Intensive care	Intensive care medicine or critical care medicine is a branch of medicine concerned with the provision of life support or organ support systems in patients who are critically ill and who usually require intensive monitoring. Patients requiring intensive care may require support for hemodynamic instability (hypertension/hypotension), airway or respiratory compromise (such as ventilator support), acute renal failure, potentially lethal cardiac arrhythmias, or the cumulative effects of multiple organ system failure. They may also be admitted for intensive/invasive monitoring, such as the crucial hours after major surgery when deemed too unstable to transfer to a less intensively monitored unit.

245

Chapter 18. Leininger's Theory of Culture Care Diversity

Theological anthropology	Theological anthropology is the branch of theology which is concerned with the study of humankind, in relation to the divine. In a theological context, it is usually referred to simply as anthropology. The Pontifical John Paul II Institute for Studies on Marriage and Family, the central session of which is held at the Pontifical Lateran University in Rome, encompasses aspects of Theological anthropology.
Blend	In linguistics, a Blend is a word formed from parts of two or more other words. These parts are sometimes, but not always, morphemes.
	Blends deal with the action of abridging and then combining various lexemes to form a new word.
Cardiac	The heart is a muscular organ found in all vertebrates that is responsible for pumping blood throughout the blood vessels by repeated, rhythmic contractions. The term cardiac means 'related to the heart' and comes from the Greek καρδιῑ¬, kardia, for 'heart.'
	The vertebrate heart is composed of cardiac muscle, which is an involuntary striated muscle tissue found only within this organ. The average human heart, beating at 72 beats per minute, will beat approximately 2.5 billion times during an average 66 year lifespan.
Nursing	Nursing is a healthcare profession focused on the care of individuals, families, and communities so they may attain, maintain, or recover optimal health and quality of life from conception to death.
	Nurses work in a large variety of specialties where they work independently and as part of a team to assess, plan, implement and evaluate care. Nursing Science is a field of knowledge based on the contributions of nursing scientist through peer reviewed scholarly journals and evidenced-based practice.
Theory	Originally the word theory is a technical term from Ancient Greek. It is derived from theoria, θεωρ?α, meaning "a looking at, viewing, beholding", and refers to contemplation or speculation, as opposed to action. Theory is especially often contrasted to "practice" a concept that in its original Aristotelian context referred to actions done for their own sake, but can also refer to "technical" actions instrumental to some other aim, such as the making of tools or houses.

Chapter 18. Leininger's Theory of Culture Care Diversity

Nurse	A Nurse is a healthcare professional who, in collaboration with other members of a health care team, is responsible for: treatment, safety, and recovery of acutely or chronically ill individuals; health promotion and maintenance within families, communities and populations; and, treatment of life-threatening emergencies in a wide range of health care settings. Nurses perform a wide range of clinical and non-clinical functions necessary to the delivery of health care, and may also be involved in medical and nursing research. Both Nursing roles and education were first defined by Florence Nightingale, following her experiences caring for the wounded in the Crimean War.
Generic	Generic is something that is general, common, or inclusive rather than specific, unique, or selective. · Generic mood, a grammatical mood used to make generalized statements like Snow is white · Generic antecedents, referents in linguistic contexts, which are classes · Generic role-playing game system, a framework that provides rule mechanics for any setting--world or environment or genre · Generic drug, a drug identified by its chemical name rather than its brand name In computer programming: · Generic function, a computer programming entity made up of all methods having the same name · Generic programming, a computer programming technique that allows a method/function or class to be defined, irrespective of the concrete data types used upon instantiation · Generic!Artemis, a computer virus

In mathematics:

· Generic filter, a mathematical filter that satisfies certain properties

· Generic point, a special kind of point whose behavior reflects the behavior of a closed subset of an algebraic variety or scheme

· Generic property, a formal definition of a property shared by almost all objects of a certain type

· Generic formalism, a mathematical framework to describe irreversible phenomena in thermodynamics

In business:

· Generic brand, a brand for a product that does not have an associated brand or trademark other than the trading name of the business providing the product

· Genericized trademark, a trademark that sometimes or usually replaces a common term in colloquial usage

· Porter Generic strategies, a category scheme of business strategies

· Semi-Generic, a term used in the United States for certain wine designations that hold no legal meaning

In zoology:

· anything pertaining to a genus

In music:

Chapter 18. Leininger's Theory of Culture Care Diversity

	· Album - Generic Flipper
	· The Advantage, an American band originally called Generic
Anxiety	Anxiety is a psychological and physiological state characterized by somatic, emotional, cognitive, and behavioral components. The root meaning of the word anxiety is 'to vex or trouble'; in either the absence or presence of psychological stress, anxiety can create feelings of fear, worry, uneasiness and dread. Anxiety is considered to be a normal reaction to stress.
Contemporary	Contemporary history describes the historical timeframe that are immediately relevant to the present and is a certain perspective of modern history.
	Recent contemporary history's intentionally loose definition includes major events such as the World War II, but not those events whose effects have been overcome.The word contemporary also means the moderns styles of today's era.
	contemporary historic events are immediately relevant to the present day.
Tachycardia	Tachycardia comes from the Greek words tachys (rapid or accelerated) and kardia (of the heart). Tachycardia typically refers to a heart rate that exceeds the normal range for a resting heartrate (heartrate in an inactive or sleeping individual). It can be dangerous depending on the speed and type of rhythm.
Heart	The Heart is one of the zàng organs stipulated by Traditional Chinese Medicine (TCM). It is a functionally defined entity and not equivalent to the anatomical organ of the same name.
	In the context of the zang-fu concept
	As a zàng, the Heart is considered to be a yin organ.

Chapter 18. Leininger's Theory of Culture Care Diversity

Nursing theory	Nursing theory is the term given to the body of knowledge that is used to define or explain various aspects of the profession of nursing. Types of nursing theories Grand nursing theories Grand nursing theories have the broadest scope and present general concepts and propositions. Theories at this level may both reflect and provide insights useful for practice but are not designed for empirical testing.
Amish	The various Amish Mennonite church fellowships are Christian religious denominations that form a very traditional subgrouping of Mennonite churches. The Amish are known for simple living, plain dress, and reluctance to adopt modern convenience. The history of the Amish church began with a schism in Switzerland within a group of Swiss and Alsatian Anabaptists in 1693 led by Jakob Ammann.
Family	Family is a group of people or animals (many species form the equivalent of a human Family wherein the adults care for the young) affiliated by consanguinity, affinity or co-residence. Although the concept of consanguinity originally referred to relations by `blood`, anthropologists have argued that one must understand the idea of `blood` metaphorically and that many societies understand Family through other concepts rather than through genetic distance. One of the primary functions of the Family is to produce and reproduce persons, biologically and socially.
Assessment	Educational Assessment is the process of documenting, usually in measurable terms, knowledge, skills, attitudes and beliefs. Assessment can focus on the individual learner, the learning community (class, workshop, or other organized group of learners), the institution, or the educational system as a whole. According to the Academic Exchange Quarterly: 'Studies of a theoretical or empirical nature addressing the Assessment of learner aptitude and preparation, motivation and learning styles, learning outcomes in achievement and satisfaction in different educational contexts are all welcome, as are studies addressing issues of measurable standards and benchmarks'.

Chapter 18. Leininger`s Theory of Culture Care Diversity

Adaptation	Adaptation is the process whereby a population becomes better suited to its habitat. This process takes place over many generations, and is one of the basic phenomena of biology. The significance of an Adaptation can only be understood in relation to the total biology of the species.
Case study	A case study is a research method common in social science. It is based on an in-depth investigation of a single individual, group, or event. Case studies may be descriptive or explanatory.
Nutrition	Nutrition is the provision, to cells and organisms, of the materials necessary (in the form of food) to support life. Many common health problems can be prevented or alleviated with a healthy diet. Overview Nutrition science investigates the metabolic and physiological responses of the body to diet.
Blood	Blood is a specialized bodily fluid that delivers necessary substances to the body's cells -- such as nutrients and oxygen -- and transports waste products away from those same cells. In vertebrates, it is composed of Blood cells suspended in a liquid called Blood plasma. Plasma, which comprises 55% of Blood fluid, is mostly water (90% by volume), and contains dissolved proteins, glucose, mineral ions, hormones, carbon dioxide (plasma being the main medium for excretory product transportation), platelets and Blood cells themselves.
Experience	Experience as a general concept comprises knowledge of or skill in or observation of some thing or some event gained through involvement in or exposure to that thing or event. The history of the word experience aligns it closely with the concept of experiment. The concept of experience generally refers to know-how or procedural knowledge, rather than propositional knowledge: on-the-job training rather than book-learning.

257

Chapter 18. Leininger`s Theory of Culture Care Diversity

Hare Krishna	The Hare Krishna mantra, also referred to reverentially as the Maha Mantra ("Great Mantra"), is a sixteen-word Vaishnava mantra which first appeared in the Kali-Santarana Upanishad, and which from the 15th century rose to importance in the Bhakti movement following the teachings of Chaitanya Mahaprabhu. According to Gaudiya Vaishnava theology, one's original consciousness and goal of life is pure love of God (Krishna). Since the 1960s, the mantra has been made well known outside of India by A. C. Bhaktivedanta Swami Prabhupada and his International Society for Krishna Consciousness (commonly known as "the Hare Krishnas").
Social	The term Social refers to a characteristic of living organisms (humans in particular, though biologists also apply the term to populations of other animals). It always refers to the interaction of organisms with other organisms and to their collective co-existence, irrespective of whether they are aware of it or not, and irrespective of whether the interaction is voluntary or involuntary. In the absence of agreement about its meaning, the term `Social` is used in many different senses and regarded as a fuzzy concept, referring among other things to: · Attitudes, orientations, or behaviours which take the interests, intentions, or needs of other people into account (in contrast to anti-Social behaviour);has played some role in defining the idea or the principle. For instance terms like Social realism, Social justice, Social constructivism, Social psychology and Social capital imply that there is some Social process involved or considered, a process that is not there in regular, `non-Social`, realism, justice, constructivism, psychology, or capital.
Breastfeeding	Breastfeeding is the feeding of an infant or young child with breast milk directly from female human breasts (i.e., via lactation) rather than from a baby bottle or other container. Babies have a sucking reflex that enables them to suck and swallow milk. Most mothers can breastfeed for six months or more, without the addition of infant formula or solid food.
Accommodation	Accommodation is the process by which the vertebrate eye changes optical power to maintain a clear image (focus) on an object as its distance changes.

Accommodation acts like a reflex, but can also be consciously controlled. Mammals, birds and reptiles vary the optical power by changing the form of the elastic lens using the ciliary body (in humans up to 15 diopters).

Chapter 19. Parse`s Theory of Humanbecoming in Nursing Practice,

Theory	Originally the word theory is a technical term from Ancient Greek. It is derived from theoria, θεωρ? α, meaning "a looking at, viewing, beholding", and refers to contemplation or speculation, as opposed to action. Theory is especially often contrasted to "practice" a concept that in its original Aristotelian context referred to actions done for their own sake, but can also refer to "technical" actions instrumental to some other aim, such as the making of tools or houses.
Nursing	Nursing is a healthcare profession focused on the care of individuals, families, and communities so they may attain, maintain, or recover optimal health and quality of life from conception to death. Nurses work in a large variety of specialties where they work independently and as part of a team to assess, plan, implement and evaluate care. Nursing Science is a field of knowledge based on the contributions of nursing scientist through peer reviewed scholarly journals and evidenced-based practice.
Nursing Theory	Nursing theory is the term given to the body of knowledge that is used to define or explain various aspects of the profession of nursing. Types of nursing theories Grand nursing theories Grand nursing theories have the broadest scope and present general concepts and propositions. Theories at this level may both reflect and provide insights useful for practice but are not designed for empirical testing.
Utilization	Utilization is a statistical concept (Queueing Theory) as well as a primary business measure for the rental industry. In queueing theory, utilization is the proportion of the system`s resources which is used by the traffic which arrives at it. It should be strictly less than one for the system to function well.

CIam101

Chapter 19. Parse`s Theory of Humanbecoming in Nursing Practice,

Education	Education in the largest sense is any act or experience that has a formative effect on the mind, character or physical ability of an individual. In its technical sense, education is the process by which society deliberately transmits its accumulated knowledge, skills and values from one generation to another. Etymologically, the word education is derived from educare "bring up", which is related to educere "bring out", "bring forth what is within", "bring out potential" and ducere, "to lead".
Critique	Critique is a method of disciplined, systematic analysis of a written or oral discourse. Critique is an accepted format of written and oral debate. Critique differs from (is not) criticism in that critique is never personalized nor ad hominem, but is instead the analyses of the structure of the thought in the content of the item critiqued.
Humans	Humans commonly refers to the species Homo sapiens , the only extant member of the Homo genus of bipedal primates in Hominidae, the great ape family. However, in some cases the term is used to refer to any member of the genus Homo. Humans have a highly developed brain, capable of abstract reasoning, language, introspection, and problem solving.
Major	Major is a rank of commissioned officer, with corresponding ranks existing in almost every military in the world. When used unhyphenated, in conjunction with no other indicator of rank, the term refers to the rank just senior to that of an Army captain and just below the rank of lieutenant colonel. It is considered the most junior of the field ranks.
Nursing research	Nursing research is the term used to describe the evidence used to support nursing practice. Nursing, as an evidence based area of practice, has been developing since the time of Florence Nightingale to the present day, where many nurses now work as researchers based in universities as well as in the health care setting.

CTAM101

Chapter 19. Parse`s Theory of Humanbecoming in Nursing Practice,

Nurse education places emphasis upon the use of evidence from research in order to rationalise nursing interventions.

Paradigm

The word paradigm has been used in science to describe distinct concepts. It comes from Greek "παρ?δειγμα" (paradeigma), "pattern, example, sample" from the verb "παραδε?κνυμι" (paradeiknumi), "exhibit, represent, expose" and that from "παρ?" (para), "beside, by" + "δε?κνυμι" (deiknumi), "to show, to point out".

The original Greek term παραδε?γματι (paradeigma) was used in Greek texts such as Plato's Timaeus (28A) as the model or the pattern that the Demiurge (god) used to create the cosmos.

Telerobotics

Telerobotics is the area of robotics concerned with the control of robots from a distance, chiefly using wireless connections (like Wi-Fi, Bluetooth, the Deep Space Network, and similar), `tethered` connections, teleoperation and telepresence.
Teleoperation means `doing work at a distance`, although `work` may mean almost anything.

Theories

[For a more detailed account of theories as expressed in formal language as they are studied in mathematical logic see Theory (mathematical logic.)]
The term theory has two broad sets of meanings, one used in the empirical sciences (both natural and social) and the other used in philosophy, mathematics, logic, and across other fields in the humanities. There is considerable difference and even dispute across academic disciplines as to the proper usages of the term. What follows is an attempt to describe how the term is used, not to try to say how it ought to be used.

In Practice

In Practice is published in conjunction with The Veterinary Record and provides continuing educational material for veterinary practitioners. It focuses on the topics of clinical and practice management. Reviews cover all species, but principally farm and companion animals, providing a regular update on clinical developments.

Paradox

A paradox is a seemingly true statement or group of statements that lead to a contradiction or a situation which seems to defy logic or intuition. The term is also used for an apparent contradiction that actually expresses a non-dual truth such as two true sentences which put together seem incompatible as both being true (cf. Catuskoti).

Chapter 19. Parse`s Theory of Humanbecoming in Nursing Practice,

Imaging	Imaging is the representation or reproduction of an object`s outward form; especially a visual representation (i.e., the formation of an image). · Chemical Imaging, the simultaneous measurement of spectra and pictures · Creation of a disk image, a file which contains the exact content of a non-volatile computer data storage medium.
Health	At the time of the creation of the World Health Organization (WHO), in 1948, Health was defined as being `a state of complete physical, mental, and social well-being and not merely the absence of disease or infirmity`. This definition invited nations to expand the conceptual framework of their Health systems beyond issues related to the physical condition of individuals and their diseases, and it motivated us to focus our attention on what we now call social determinants of Health. Consequently, WHO challenged political, academic, community, and professional organizations devoted to improving or preserving Health to make the scope of their work explicit, including their rationale for allocating resources.
Process and Reality	In philosophy, especially metaphysics, the book Process and Reality by Alfred North Whitehead sets out its author`s philosophy of organism published in 1929, is a revision of the Gifford Lectures he gave in 1927-28. Process philosophy lays the groundwork for a paradigm of subjectivity, which Whitehead calls a `completed metaphysical language.` (p.
Case study	A case study is a research method common in social science. It is based on an in-depth investigation of a single individual, group, or event. Case studies may be descriptive or explanatory.

Chapter 20. Newman`s Theory of Health as Expanding Consciousness in Nursing,

Health	At the time of the creation of the World Health Organization (WHO), in 1948, Health was defined as being `a state of complete physical, mental, and social well-being and not merely the absence of disease or infirmity`.
	This definition invited nations to expand the conceptual framework of their Health systems beyond issues related to the physical condition of individuals and their diseases, and it motivated us to focus our attention on what we now call social determinants of Health. Consequently, WHO challenged political, academic, community, and professional organizations devoted to improving or preserving Health to make the scope of their work explicit, including their rationale for allocating resources.
Theory	Originally the word theory is a technical term from Ancient Greek. It is derived from theoria, θεωρ?α, meaning "a looking at, viewing, beholding", and refers to contemplation or speculation, as opposed to action. Theory is especially often contrasted to "practice" a concept that in its original Aristotelian context referred to actions done for their own sake, but can also refer to "technical" actions instrumental to some other aim, such as the making of tools or houses.
Education	Education in the largest sense is any act or experience that has a formative effect on the mind, character or physical ability of an individual. In its technical sense, education is the process by which society deliberately transmits its accumulated knowledge, skills and values from one generation to another.
	Etymologically, the word education is derived from educare "bring up", which is related to educere "bring out", "bring forth what is within", "bring out potential" and ducere, "to lead".
Healing	Physiological healing is the restoration of damaged living tissue to normal function. It is the process by which the cells in the body regenerate and repair to reduce the size of a damaged or necrotic area. Healing incorporates both the removal of necrotic tissue (demolition), and the replacement of this tissue.
In Practice	In Practice is published in conjunction with The Veterinary Record and provides continuing educational material for veterinary practitioners. It focuses on the topics of clinical and practice management. Reviews cover all species, but principally farm and companion animals, providing a regular update on clinical developments.

Chapter 20. Newman's Theory of Health as Expanding Consciousness in Nursing,

Nursing	Nursing is a healthcare profession focused on the care of individuals, families, and communities so they may attain, maintain, or recover optimal health and quality of life from conception to death.
	Nurses work in a large variety of specialties where they work independently and as part of a team to assess, plan, implement and evaluate care. Nursing Science is a field of knowledge based on the contributions of nursing scientist through peer reviewed scholarly journals and evidenced-based practice.
Wound	In medicine, a wound is a type of injury in which skin is torn, cut or punctured (an open wound), or where blunt force trauma causes a contusion (a closed wound). In pathology, it specifically refers to a sharp injury which damages the dermis of the skin.
	Classification
	Open
	Open wounds can be classified according to the object that caused the wound.
Wound healing	Wound healing, is an intricate process in which the skin (or another organ-tissue) repairs itself after injury. In normal skin, the epidermis (outermost layer) and dermis (inner or deeper layer) exists in a steady-state equilibrium, forming a protective barrier against the external environment. Once the protective barrier is broken, the normal (physiologic) process of wound healing is immediately set in motion.
Evolution	Evolution is the change in the inherited traits of a population of organisms through successive generations. After a population splits into smaller groups, these groups evolve independently and may eventually diversify into new species. A nested hierarchy of anatomical and genetic similarities, geographical distribution of similar species and the fossil record indicate that all organisms are descended from a common ancestor through a long series of these divergent events, stretching back in a tree of life that has grown over the 3,500 million years of life on Earth.

Chapter 20. Newman's Theory of Health as Expanding Consciousness in Nursing,

Humans	Humans commonly refers to the species Homo sapiens , the only extant member of the Homo genus of bipedal primates in Hominidae, the great ape family. However, in some cases the term is used to refer to any member of the genus Homo.
	Humans have a highly developed brain, capable of abstract reasoning, language, introspection, and problem solving.
Timing	Timing is the spacing of events in time. Some typical uses are:
	· The act of measuring the elapsed time of something or someone, often at athletic events such as swimming or running, where participants are timed with a device such as a stopwatch.
	· Engine Timing, for various functions such as ignition, cam Timing to control poppet valve Timing and overlap, and fuel injection Timing.
	· see ignition Timing
	· Timing light,
	· Timing mark
	· Comic Timing by a comedian or actor, an element of humor.
	· In phonology, the rhythm of a spoken language.
Case study	A case study is a research method common in social science. It is based on an in-depth investigation of a single individual, group, or event. Case studies may be descriptive or explanatory.

Chapter 20. Newman`s Theory of Health as Expanding Consciousness in Nursing,

Family	Family is a group of people or animals (many species form the equivalent of a human Family wherein the adults care for the young) affiliated by consanguinity, affinity or co-residence. Although the concept of consanguinity originally referred to relations by `blood`, anthropologists have argued that one must understand the idea of `blood` metaphorically and that many societies understand Family through other concepts rather than through genetic distance. One of the primary functions of the Family is to produce and reproduce persons, biologically and socially.
Assessment	Educational Assessment is the process of documenting, usually in measurable terms, knowledge, skills, attitudes and beliefs. Assessment can focus on the individual learner, the learning community (class, workshop, or other organized group of learners), the institution, or the educational system as a whole. According to the Academic Exchange Quarterly: 'Studies of a theoretical or empirical nature addressing the Assessment of learner aptitude and preparation, motivation and learning styles, learning outcomes in achievement and satisfaction in different educational contexts are all welcome, as are studies addressing issues of measurable standards and benchmarks'.
Customer	A customer buyer, is usually used to refer to a current or potential buyer or user of the products of an individual or organization, called the supplier, seller, or vendor. This is typically through purchasing or renting goods or services. However, in certain contexts, the term customer also includes by extension anyone who uses or experiences the services of another.
String searching algorithms	String searching algorithms are an important class of string algorithms that try to find a place where one or several strings are found within a larger string or text. Let Σ be an alphabet (finite set). Formally, both the pattern and searched text are concatenations of elements of Σ.
Disease	A disease is an abnormal condition affecting the body of an organism. It is often construed to be a medical condition associated with specific symptoms and signs. It may be caused by external factors, such as infectious disease, or it may be caused by internal dysfunctions, such as autoimmune diseases.

Chapter 21. Areas for Further Development of Theory-Based Nursing Practice,

Nursing	Nursing is a healthcare profession focused on the care of individuals, families, and communities so they may attain, maintain, or recover optimal health and quality of life from conception to death.
	Nurses work in a large variety of specialties where they work independently and as part of a team to assess, plan, implement and evaluate care. Nursing Science is a field of knowledge based on the contributions of nursing scientist through peer reviewed scholarly journals and evidenced-based practice.
Nursing theory	Nursing theory is the term given to the body of knowledge that is used to define or explain various aspects of the profession of nursing.
	Types of nursing theories
	Grand nursing theories
	Grand nursing theories have the broadest scope and present general concepts and propositions. Theories at this level may both reflect and provide insights useful for practice but are not designed for empirical testing.
Education	Education in the largest sense is any act or experience that has a formative effect on the mind, character or physical ability of an individual. In its technical sense, education is the process by which society deliberately transmits its accumulated knowledge, skills and values from one generation to another.
	Etymologically, the word education is derived from educare "bring up", which is related to educere "bring out", "bring forth what is within", "bring out potential" and ducere, "to lead".

Go to **Cram101.com** for Interactive Practice Exams for this book or virtually any of your books.
And, **NEVER** highlight a book again!

Chapter 21. Areas for Further Development of Theory-Based Nursing Practice,

Knowledge	Knowledge is defined by the Oxford English Dictionary as (i) expertise, and skills acquired by a person through experience or education; the theoretical or practical understanding of a subject; (ii) what is known in a particular field or in total; facts and information; or (iii) be absolutely certain or sure about something. Philosophical debates in general start with Plato's formulation of knowledge as "justified true belief." There is however no single agreed definition of knowledge presently, nor any prospect of one, and there remain numerous competing theories. Knowledge acquisition involves complex cognitive processes: perception, learning, communication, association and reasoning.
Theory	Originally the word theory is a technical term from Ancient Greek. It is derived from theoria, θεωρ? α, meaning "a looking at, viewing, beholding", and refers to contemplation or speculation, as opposed to action. Theory is especially often contrasted to "practice" a concept that in its original Aristotelian context referred to actions done for their own sake, but can also refer to "technical" actions instrumental to some other aim, such as the making of tools or houses.
Humans	Humans commonly refers to the species Homo sapiens , the only extant member of the Homo genus of bipedal primates in Hominidae, the great ape family. However, in some cases the term is used to refer to any member of the genus Homo.
	Humans have a highly developed brain, capable of abstract reasoning, language, introspection, and problem solving.
Science of Unitary Human Beings	The science of unitary human beings is a grand nursing theory developed by Martha E. Rogers. The details of the theory are included in her book, An Introduction to the Theoretical Basis of Nursing.
	Overview
	According to Rogers, Nursing is both a science and an art.
Self-Care Deficit Nursing Theory	The self-care deficit nursing theory is a grand nursing theory that was developed between 1959 and 2001 by Dorothea Orem. It is also known as the Orem model of nursing. It is particularly used in rehabilitation and primary care settings where the patient is encouraged to be as independent as possible.
Theories	[For a more detailed account of theories as expressed in formal language as they are studied in mathematical logic see Theory (mathematical logic)]

Chapter 21. Areas for Further Development of Theory-Based Nursing Practice,

	The term theory has two broad sets of meanings, one used in the empirical sciences (both natural and social) and the other used in philosophy, mathematics, logic, and across other fields in the humanities. There is considerable difference and even dispute across academic disciplines as to the proper usages of the term. What follows is an attempt to describe how the term is used, not to try to say how it ought to be used.
Adaptation	Adaptation is the process whereby a population becomes better suited to its habitat. This process takes place over many generations, and is one of the basic phenomena of biology.
	The significance of an Adaptation can only be understood in relation to the total biology of the species.
Health	At the time of the creation of the World Health Organization (WHO), in 1948, Health was defined as being `a state of complete physical, mental, and social well-being and not merely the absence of disease or infirmity`.
	This definition invited nations to expand the conceptual framework of their Health systems beyond issues related to the physical condition of individuals and their diseases, and it motivated us to focus our attention on what we now call social determinants of Health. Consequently, WHO challenged political, academic, community, and professional organizations devoted to improving or preserving Health to make the scope of their work explicit, including their rationale for allocating resources.
Nursing Process	The nursing process is a process by which nurses deliver care to individuals, families, and/or communities and is supported by nursing theories. The nursing process was originally an adapted form of problem-solving and is classified as a deductive theory.
	Phases of the nursing process
	The nursing process is a client-centered, goal-oriented method of caring that provides a framework to nursing care.
Data analysis	Analysis of data is a process of inspecting, cleaning, transforming, and modeling data with the goal of highlighting useful information, suggesting conclusions, and supporting decision making. Data analysis has multiple facets and approaches, encompassing diverse techniques under a variety of names, in different business, science, and social science domains.

Chapter 21. Areas for Further Development of Theory-Based Nursing Practice,

	Data mining is a particular data analysis technique that focuses on modeling and knowledge discovery for predictive rather than purely descriptive purposes.
Impression	A dental impression may be described as an accurate representation of part or all of a person's dentition and other areas of the mouth. The dental impression forms an imprint (i.e. a 'negative' mould) of those teeth and gums, which can then be used to make a cast or 'positive' model of the dentition. This may be used for the fabrication of dentures, crowns or other prostheses.

Chapter 22. Nursing Philosophies, Models, and Theories: A Focus on the Future,

Nursing	Nursing is a healthcare profession focused on the care of individuals, families, and communities so they may attain, maintain, or recover optimal health and quality of life from conception to death.
	Nurses work in a large variety of specialties where they work independently and as part of a team to assess, plan, implement and evaluate care. Nursing Science is a field of knowledge based on the contributions of nursing scientist through peer reviewed scholarly journals and evidenced-based practice.
Nursing theory	Nursing theory is the term given to the body of knowledge that is used to define or explain various aspects of the profession of nursing.
	Types of nursing theories
	Grand nursing theories
	Grand nursing theories have the broadest scope and present general concepts and propositions. Theories at this level may both reflect and provide insights useful for practice but are not designed for empirical testing.
Knowledge	Knowledge is defined by the Oxford English Dictionary as (i) expertise, and skills acquired by a person through experience or education; the theoretical or practical understanding of a subject; (ii) what is known in a particular field or in total; facts and information; or (iii) be absolutely certain or sure about something. Philosophical debates in general start with Plato's formulation of knowledge as "justified true belief." There is however no single agreed definition of knowledge presently, nor any prospect of one, and there remain numerous competing theories. Knowledge acquisition involves complex cognitive processes: perception, learning, communication, association and reasoning.

Chapter 22. Nursing Philosophies, Models, and Theories: A Focus on the Future,

Nurse	A Nurse is a healthcare professional who, in collaboration with other members of a health care team, is responsible for: treatment, safety, and recovery of acutely or chronically ill individuals; health promotion and maintenance within families, communities and populations; and, treatment of life-threatening emergencies in a wide range of health care settings. Nurses perform a wide range of clinical and non-clinical functions necessary to the delivery of health care, and may also be involved in medical and nursing research.
	Both Nursing roles and education were first defined by Florence Nightingale, following her experiences caring for the wounded in the Crimean War.
Nurse practitioner	A Nurse Practitioner is an Advanced Practice Nurse (APN) who has completed graduate-level education (either a Master's or a Doctoral degree). Additional APN roles include the Certified Registered Nurse Anesthetist (CRNA)s, CNMs, and CNSs. All Nurse Practitioners are Registered Nurses who have completed extensive additional education, training, and have a dramatically expanded scope of practice over the traditional RN role.
Nursing practice	Nursing practice is the actual provision of nursing care. In providing care, nurses are implementing the nursing care plan which is based on the client`s initial assessment. This is based around a specific nursing theory which will be selected as appropriate for the care setting.
Theory	Originally the word theory is a technical term from Ancient Greek. It is derived from theoria, θεωρ?α, meaning "a looking at, viewing, beholding", and refers to contemplation or speculation, as opposed to action. Theory is especially often contrasted to "practice" a concept that in its original Aristotelian context referred to actions done for their own sake, but can also refer to "technical" actions instrumental to some other aim, such as the making of tools or houses.
Vulnerability	Vulnerability refers to the susceptibility of a person, group, society or system to physical or emotional injury or attack. The term can also refer to a person who lets their guard down, leaving themselves open to censure or criticism. Vulnerability refers to a person's state of being liable to succumb to manipulation, persuasion, temptation etc.
Disease	A disease is an abnormal condition affecting the body of an organism. It is often construed to be a medical condition associated with specific symptoms and signs. It may be caused by external factors, such as infectious disease, or it may be caused by internal dysfunctions, such as autoimmune diseases.

Chapter 22. Nursing Philosophies, Models, and Theories: A Focus on the Future,

Nursing Process	The nursing process is a process by which nurses deliver care to individuals, families, and/or communities and is supported by nursing theories. The nursing process was originally an adapted form of problem-solving and is classified as a deductive theory.
	Phases of the nursing process
	The nursing process is a client-centered, goal-oriented method of caring that provides a framework to nursing care.
Synthesis	In general, the noun Synthesis refers to the combining of two or more entities to form something new. The corresponding verb, to Synthesise , means to make or form a Synthesis.
	Synthesis or Synthesise may also refer to:
	· Chemical Synthesis, the execution of chemical reactions to form a more complex molecule from chemical precursors
	· Organic Synthesis, the chemical Synthesis of organic compounds
	· Total Synthesis, the complete organic Synthesis of complex organic compounds, usually without the aid of biological processes
	· Convergent Synthesis or linear Synthesis, a strategy to improve the efficiency of multi-step chemical syntheses
	· Dehydration Synthesis, a chemical Synthesis resulting in the loss of a water molecule
	· BioSynthesis, the creation of an organic compound in a living organism, usually aided by enzymes

291

Chapter 22. Nursing Philosophies, Models, and Theories: A Focus on the Future,

· PhotoSynthesis, a biochemical reaction using a carbon molecule to produce an organic molecule, using sunlight as a catalyst

· ChemoSynthesis, the Synthesis of biological compounds into organic waste, using methane or an oxidized molecule as a catalyst

· Amino acid Synthesis, the Synthesis of an amino acid from its constituents*

· Peptide Synthesis, the biochemical Synthesis of peptides using amino acids

· Protein bioSynthesis, the multi-step biochemical Synthesis of proteins (long peptides)

· DNA Synthesis several biochemical processes for making DNA

· DNA replication, DNA bioSynthesis in vivo

· RNA Synthesis, the Synthesis of RNA from nucleic acids, using another nucleic acid chain as a template

· ATP Synthesis, the biochemical Synthesis of ATP

·

· [tyler wayne covington is the hottest motocrosser everrrrrr!]

· the process of converting a higher-level form of a design into a lower-level implementation

· Logic Synthesis

Chapter 22. Nursing Philosophies, Models, and Theories: A Focus on the Future,

· High-level Synthesis

· Sound Synthesis, various methods of sound generation in audio electronics

· Subtractive Synthesis

· Frequency modulation Synthesis

· Speech Synthesis, the artificial production of human speech

· in philosophy, the end result of a dialectic, as in thesis, antithesis, Synthesis

· a cognitive skill in Benjamin Bloom`s Taxonomy of Educational Objectives.

· In philosophy and science, a higher a priori process than analysis

· Synthesis a web site and magazine covering popular culture

· Synthesis a journal of chemical Synthesis. .

Perspective	Perspective, in context of vision and visual perception, is the way in which objects appear to the eye based on their spatial attributes; or their dimensions and the position of the eye relative to the objects. There are two main meanings of the term: linear perspective and aerial perspective.
	Linear perspective
	As objects become more distant they appear smaller because their visual angle decreases.

Chapter 22. Nursing Philosophies, Models, and Theories: A Focus on the Future,

Transformation	In molecular biology, transformation is the genetic alteration of a cell resulting from the uptake, genomic incorporation, and expression of environmental genetic material (DNA). Transformation ransformation occurs most commonly in bacteria, both naturally and artificially, and refers to DNA taken up from the environment through their cell wall. Bacteria that are capable of being transformed are called competent.
Patient care	Patient care is part of a nurse's role. Nurses use the nursing process to assess, plan, implement and evaluate Patient care Patient care is founded in critical thinking and caring in a holistic framework.
Contemporary	Contemporary history describes the historical timeframe that are immediately relevant to the present and is a certain perspective of modern history. Recent contemporary history's intentionally loose definition includes major events such as the World War II, but not those events whose effects have been overcome.The word contemporary also means the moderns styles of today's era. contemporary historic events are immediately relevant to the present day.
Humans	Humans commonly refers to the species Homo sapiens , the only extant member of the Homo genus of bipedal primates in Hominidae, the great ape family. However, in some cases the term is used to refer to any member of the genus Homo. Humans have a highly developed brain, capable of abstract reasoning, language, introspection, and problem solving.
Science of Unitary Human Beings	The science of unitary human beings is a grand nursing theory developed by Martha E. Rogers. The details of the theory are included in her book, An Introduction to the Theoretical Basis of Nursing. Overview According to Rogers, Nursing is both a science and an art.

Chapter 22. Nursing Philosophies, Models, and Theories: A Focus on the Future,

Theories	[For a more detailed account of theories as expressed in formal language as they are studied in mathematical logic see Theory (mathematical logic.)] The term theory has two broad sets of meanings, one used in the empirical sciences (both natural and social) and the other used in philosophy, mathematics, logic, and across other fields in the humanities. There is considerable difference and even dispute across academic disciplines as to the proper usages of the term. What follows is an attempt to describe how the term is used, not to try to say how it ought to be used.
Scope	Scope is a London-based charity, which operates in England and Wales, focusing on people with cerebral palsy particularly, and disabled people in general. Its aim is that disabled people achieve equality. Scope was founded on 9 October 1952 by Ian Dawson-Shepherd, Eric Hodgson, Alex Moira and a social worker, Jean Garwood.
Orthopedic	Orthopedic surgery or Orthopedics (also spelled orthopaedics) is the branch of surgery concerned with conditions involving the musculoskeletal system. Orthopedic surgeons use both surgical and non-surgical means to treat musculoskeletal trauma, sports injuries, degenerative diseases, infections, tumors, and congenital conditions. Nicholas Andry coined the word `orthopaedics`, derived from Greek words for orthos and paideion (`child`), when he published Orthopaedia: or the Art of Correcting and Preventing Deformities in Children in 1741.
Osteoporosis	Osteoporosis is a disease of bone that leads to an increased risk of fracture. In Osteoporosis the bone mineral density (BMD) is reduced, bone microarchitecture is disrupted, and the amount and variety of non-collagenous proteins in bone is altered. Osteoporosis is defined by the World Health Organization (WHO) in women as a bone mineral density 2.5 standard deviations below peak bone mass (20-year-old healthy female average) as measured by DXA; the term `established Osteoporosis` includes the presence of a fragility fracture.

Clam\101

Outcome	In game theory, an outcome is a set of moves or strategies taken by the players, or their payoffs resulting from the actions or strategies taken by all players. The two are complementary in that, given knowledge of the set of strategies of all players, the final state of the game is known, as are any relevant payoffs. In a game where chance or a random event is involved, the outcome is not known from only the set of strategies, but is only realized when the random event(s) are realized.
Health	At the time of the creation of the World Health Organization (WHO), in 1948, Health was defined as being `a state of complete physical, mental, and social well-being and not merely the absence of disease or infirmity`. This definition invited nations to expand the conceptual framework of their Health systems beyond issues related to the physical condition of individuals and their diseases, and it motivated us to focus our attention on what we now call social determinants of Health. Consequently, WHO challenged political, academic, community, and professional organizations devoted to improving or preserving Health to make the scope of their work explicit, including their rationale for allocating resources.
Adaptation	Adaptation is the process whereby a population becomes better suited to its habitat. This process takes place over many generations, and is one of the basic phenomena of biology. The significance of an Adaptation can only be understood in relation to the total biology of the species.
Self-Care Deficit Nursing Theory	The self-care deficit nursing theory is a grand nursing theory that was developed between 1959 and 2001 by Dorothea Orem. It is also known as the Orem model of nursing. It is particularly used in rehabilitation and primary care settings where the patient is encouraged to be as independent as possible.

CPSIA information can be obtained at www.ICGtesting.com
Printed in the USA
LVOW09s1344230614

391261LV00005B/485/P